Foreign Exchange Risk and Direct Foreign Investment

Research for Business Decisions, No. 60

Richard N. Farmer, Series Editor

Professor of International Business
Indiana University

Other Titles in This Series

No. 54   *Retailing Strategies for Generic Brand Grocery Products*
                                                            Jon M. Hawes

No. 55   *An Empirical Evaluation of FASB 33,* Financial Reporting and Changing Prices
                                                    Jalaleddin Soroosh Joo

No. 56   *Inventories and Foreign Currency Translation Requirements*
                                            Kathleen Ranney Bindon

No. 57   *Power Base Attribution and the Perceived Legitimacy of Managerial Accounting*
                                                    Roger W. Bartlett

No. 58   *Municipal Financial Disclosure: An Empirical Investigation*
                                            Julia Halcomb Magann

No. 59   *Auditor Risk and Legal Liability*   Kent E. St. Pierre

No. 61   *Measurement Error and Banks' Reported Earnings*
                                                    Reed McKnight

Foreign Exchange Risk and Direct Foreign Investment

by
Michael H. Siegel

UMI RESEARCH PRESS

Ann Arbor, Michigan

Produced and distributed by
UMI Research Press
an imprint of
University Microfilms International
Ann Arbor, Michigan 48106

Library of Congress Cataloging in Publication Data

Siegel, Michael H.
　Foreign exchange risk and direct foreign
investment.

　　(Research for business decisions ; no. 60)
　　Revision of thesis, The University of Michigan, 1981.
　　Bibliography: p.
　　Includes index.
　　1. Foreign exchange problem. 2. Investments–Foreign.
3. International business enterprises–Finance. I. Title.
II. Series.

HG3852.S53　1983　　　658.1'5　　　　　83-1097
ISBN 0-8357-1398-9

Contents

List of Figures   *vii*

List of Tables   *ix*

Acknowledgments   *xi*

1   Introduction   *1*
      Introduction
      Research Motivation
      Basis of the Problem
      Exchange-Risk Exposure
      Outline and Scope of Study

2   Review of the Literature   *7*
      Introduction
      Existing Models of Exchange Risk and Direct Investment
      Summary

3   Exchange Risk   *15*
      Introduction
      Accounting Risk
      Economic Risk
      Summary

4   Exchange Risk and the Investment Decision   *27*
      Introduction
      Theoretical Model
      Interpretation of First-Order Conditions
      Comparative Static Analysis
      Summary and Conclusions

5   Currency Denomination of Debt   *41*
      Introduction
      A Model of Direct Investment and Foreign-Currency Debt
      Interpretation of First-Order Conditions
      Comparative Static Results
      Summary and Conclusions

6   Exchange Risk and International Trade   *53*
      Introduction
      A Model of Exchange Risk and International Trade
      Interpretation of First-Order Conditions
      Comparative Static Results
      Summary and Conclusions

7   Summary and Conclusions   *67*

Appendix A: Second-Order Conditions for Utility
      Maximization   *71*

Appendix B: Total Derivatives   *75*

Notes   *81*

Bibliography   *89*

Index   *93*

List of Figures

1. Economic Risk When Purchasing Power Parity Holds   *20*

2. Economic Risk and Deviations from Purchasing Power Parity   *20*

3. Foreign Output Prices, Exchange Rates, and the Degree of Competition from World Markets   *22*

4. Foreign Wage Costs, Exchange Rates, and the Degree of Competition from World Markets   *23*

5. Short-Run Supply Curve for New Capital   *29*

6. Positive Correlations of $eP_2(e)$ and $eW_2(e)$ *59*

7. Negative Correlations of $eP_2(e)$ and $eW_2(e)$ *61*

List of Tables

1. Impact of Local-Currency Depreciation on Local-Currency Profit Margins   *24*

2. Comparative Static Analysis—Investment Model   *36*

3. Comparative Static Analysis—Foreign Debt Model   *52*

4. Comparative Static Analysis—Trade Model   *62*

5. Changes in the Volume of Firm-Wide Sales and Net Exports to the Foreign Market   *63*

Acknowledgments

I wish to express my appreciation to Professor Alan V. Deardorff, who provided valuable assistance on technical matters and an overall sense of direction for this study. I also wish to express my gratitude to Professor Gunter Dufey for the encouragement he gave me and the valuable time spent discussing the more subtle issues in international finance.

Acknowledgment is also given to Professors Robert Stern and John Laitner for their constructive advice and assistance. I also wish to thank Raj Aggarwal who provided key suggestions for rewriting and redirecting certain sections of the text; and Joan Mathews and Chris Weatherford for technical editing.

Finally, I wish to express my love for Susie and Aaron, and for my parents.

1

Introduction

Introduction

The late 1960s and early 1970s were witness to a lengthy period of unsettling change in the international financial markets. The United States dollar, the principal currency of the international monetary system, came under attack. The price of gold and most of the currencies of the world were expressed in terms of their exchange value for U.S. dollars. The prices of goods that trade between countries were expressed in dollars, and the dollar was the currency of settlement for virtually all transactions between trading partners. To say that the dollar was the "international medium of exchange" is not to overstate the truth.

This key role for the U.S. dollar, acting as an international currency, had served well since 1946 when the Bretton Woods agreement (Articles of Agreement of the International Monetary Fund) was signed. This agreement established the International Monetary Fund (IMF), created rules for a system of fixed rates of exchanges for currencies, and created a currency reserve for the IMF to use in its role as the international lender of the last resort.

As the decade of the 1960s progressed and the United States incurred larger and larger balance of payments deficits, the world began to find itself with too many dollars relative to its needs. The relationship of the dollar to other currencies and to gold was in need of adjustment and this required government action.

The slow reaction of key governments (United States, Germany, Japan, to name but a few) created very rewarding speculative opportunities. The markets responded and financial claims began to move through the financial markets in a very disturbing fashion. One by one, countries were forced to act. Germany revalued the mark in 1969 and again in May of 1971. Canada set its currency afloat in 1970. President Nixon suspended dollar convertibility (the exchange of dollars for gold) in August of 1971 to curb the outflow of gold encouraged by an overvalued dollar (undervalued dollar price for gold). A few months later the dollar was devalued against gold, and the major currencies of the world were revalued against the dollar. Slowly, the Bretton Woods agreement was being dismembered.

Government actions were too few too late in response to market conditions that were changing at a far faster pace. More adjustments were made, but finally in early 1973 the major currencies of the world were set afloat. The exchange value of these currencies were to be established on a trade-by-trade basis in the international financial markets.

Many economists believed that a system of floating or market-determined exchange rates would help restore exchange-rate stability. The rationale was that the markets could better determine the equilibrium exchange value or "appropriate" exchange rate for these currencies. The economists were correct in one respect, the markets were a better mechanism for setting the prices of currencies. Stability, however, did not result.

Many factors are at play in determining the equilibrium or exchange value of a currency. These factors include a country's international balance of payments, interest rates, inflation rates, the stage of the business cycle, perceptions and expectations, international competitiveness, domestic re-source availability, changing production technologies, and so on. When these factors remain stable, the rate of exchange will remain stable. To the extent that inflation rates, interest rates and the like begin to gyrate, the exchange rate, which is another price in the overall economic system, will gyrate in response.

What conclusions, if any, are to be drawn? The extreme volatility which the foreign exchange markets have experienced since the late 1960s should be expected to continue. The causes of this volatility have not changed: changing worldwide economic conditions and, in particular, shifting policy courses followed by national economies. Why should the resultant effects differ?

The volatility of exchange rates have played havoc with the domestic and international operations of multinational firms. With this volatility likely to continue in the future, an in-depth study of exchange risk and the international operations of the firm is of value. This book attempts to provide such a study with respect to international direct investment considerations.

Exchange risk is the risk that unanticipated exchange-rate changes may alter the intrinsic value of the firm. The change in value may result from gains or losses on currency holdings, changes in the value of debt, the value of inventory, or changes in the value of goods in transit. Of potentially greater concern is the effect that changing exchange rates may have on the competitive position of the firm. The firm may find that exchange-rate adjustments have altered the market for inputs to the production process, or that the market for its products may have been materially influenced by the change in the rate or exchange.

Research Motivation

The end of the fixed exchange-rate regime, in conjunction with the volatile behavior of the foreign exchange markets, directed research attention to the study of international economic behavior under conditions of uncertainty. Studies in the early 1970s focused on the effect of exchange risk on the pricing and holding of equities, financial claims, and currencies.[1] Since the mid-1970s this field of research has broadened to include the areas of exchange-rate determination, international trade, and corporate behavior.[2]

Early research on corporate behavior and exchange risk was concerned with the financial aspects of the firm to the neglect of broader economic considerations. As a result, much of the literature was devoted to discussions of "accounting risk," or the impact of exchange-rate changes on the contractual flows and balance sheet of the firm.[3] However, the effects of exchange-rate changes can be more extensive and pervasive than these "accounting" effects.[4] With few exceptions, studies of the economic effects of exchange risk on the operations, profitability and investment decisions of the firm are lacking. Issues such as the relationship between exchange risk and direct investment, export versus local production, and the currency denomination of financial liabilities have not been adequately investigated.

Past studies on exchange risk and direct investment have, in general, been deficient. Shortcomings include the misspecification of exchange risk, the use of financial models (the capital asset pricing model) to explain direct investment, and the failure to recognize the risk implications of the trade-off between capital and labor in production.

The work presented here studies the effect of exchange risk on the international investment behavior of the firm. This book addresses three related subjects: the direct investment decision, the debt-denomination decision, and the production/export decision. The main focus is on exchange risk and the related nature of these decisions with respect to exposure to exchange risk.

Basis of the Problem

In an uncertain world, profit cannot be realized without exposure to risk. Even the "risk-free" nominal return on government obligations is at risk when real rates of return are considered. The existence of risk due to uncertainty requires the risk-averse investor to consider the probability distribution of financial returns in the evaluation of investment alternatives.

Markowitz, in his 1952 pioneering article, "Portfolio Selection," first demonstrated the gains to an investor from holding a portfolio of diversified assets. Markowitz showed that a portfolio of assets whose returns are less than perfectly correlated provides equivalent returns at lower risk. This work formed the foundation of a broad field of study known as portfolio theory and its extension, called capital-market theory.

In the late 1960s and early 1970s the concept of portfolio diversification was broadened in scope. Several writers explored issues regarding the potential gains from international portfolio diversification. These writers (including Grubel [1968], Levy and Sarnat [1970], Agmon [1972, 1973], Solnik [1974], Lessard [1974, 1976], and Errunza [1977]) concluded that gains are achievable by diversifying financial asset portfolios internationally.

The observed behavior of private investors, however, contradicts the conclusions of this body of theoretical and empirical research. Private investors as a class tend to hold few foreign assets in their portfolios. Several reasons are given for the failure of investors to diversify portfolios internationally. These reasons include governmental constraints, limited information, high transaction costs, illiquid foreign markets, and exchange risk. An alternative path for investors to pursue is the purchase of shares in multinational corporations. Instead of assembling a portfolio of shares in separate companies that operate in different national markets, the investor can invest in the shares of a single company with internationally diversified operations. The purchase of shares of the multinational company thereby offers a more accessible avenue to the investor for internationally diversifying investment portfolios.

Empirical research by Hughes, Logue, and Sweeny (1975), Agmon and Lessard (1977), and Rugman (1980) supports the notion that investors recognize the diversification benefits offered by multinational corporations and reward these firms with a higher market valuation. The higher valuation indicates that investors are willing to "pay" an additional sum for the lower risks associated with internationally diversified operations. These results suggest that the multinational firm should consider real asset diversification as an objective in the corporate investment decision.[5]

This conclusion differs with capital-market theory which argues that the individual investor can most efficiently diversify asset holdings and that attempts at the level of the firm to diversify risk for the shareholder are duplicative and inefficient. If, however, barriers prevent efficient portfolio diversification by the individual, the firm then provides a service or benefit to shareholders by diversifying risk internationally through direct investment.

Portfolio gains from international diversification arise from enlarging the available asset set and, more significantly, from the diversification of business-cycle risks. When the range of possible investments is expanded from the domestic market to the world market, it is probable that some foreign investment opportunities are found to be more attractive than the best of the domestic investment choices. Including these foreign investments in the portfolio improves the portfolio's risk-return characteristics. When cyclical risks (business cycle risks) are considered, further risk-return improvements are realized by the inclusion of the foreign investments since business cycles are not fully synchronized between national economies. Obtaining these diversification gains has implicit costs, however, through the creation of exposure to political and foreign exchange risk.

Exchange-Risk Exposure

Exchange risk refers to the uncertain effect changing exchange rates have on the value and operations of the firm. Exchange-rate adjustments can affect the valuation of the firm's contracts and balance sheet (accounting exposure), as the translated value of these stocks is altered when the prevailing rate of exchange changes. Exchange-rate adjustments also affect the markets in which the firm operates (economic exposure) as relative prices and real incomes are altered. Some effects are cosmetic in nature, while other potential effects can be adequately protected against. This study is concerned with economic exchange risk, or the effects of unanticipated exchange-rate changes on the input and output markets of the firm. Changes in these markets alter revenue and cost flows and the relationship between these flows.

Economic exposure is not a uniform condition affecting all firms with international operations. Similarly, domestic firms are not consistently insulated from exchange risk. Exposure to economic risk is greatest for firms with operations in the import or export markets or markets in competition with the import or export markets. These markets are most sensitive to changes in the real rate of exchange.

The relationship of the tradable goods sector to the remainder of the economy exposes this sector to a proportionately greater burden of adjustment whenever the real rate of exchange changes.[6] A depreciating currency improves the competitive position of the tradable goods sector relative to world markets and local non-tradable goods sectors. Exports cost less when translated at a lower rate of exchange, while imports become more costly in the domestic market. The competitive position of the export producers and of the import-competing producers improves as the domestic currency depreciates. An appreciating currency has the opposite effect as the tradable goods sector becomes less competitive relative to world markets and non-tradable goods.

Firms that operate in sectors sensitive to exchange-rate movements find producer demand to be more volatile than in the insulated sectors of the economy. The effect of an exchange-rate change on the operations and value of the firm is predictable given knowledge of the firm's input and output markets. Uncertainty arises from the erratic and volatile movement of real exchange rates. The risk arising from this uncertainty is heightened by the uneven process of economic adjustment which frequently results in exchange-rate movements exceeding what would be required for long-term balance-of-payments equilibrium.

Outline and Scope of Study

Of interest to this study is the effect of exchange risk on the multinational firms' investment decision and on the related financing and trade decisions. The premise used throughout this study is that exchange risk cannot be fully protected against and should be an element of consideration in these decisions. Exposure to exchange risk does not arise from a single source. Rather the exposure is created through various elements of the firms' operations. These different sources of exposure are interrelated. A comprehensive approach to exchange-risk management should recognize these interrelationships in the planning and decision-making process.

This study begins with a review of the existing literature on exchange-risk and direct investment. This is followed by a detailed discussion of exchange-risk exposure. A model is developed which permits consideration of expected returns and the variance-covariance structure of returns in the investment decision. Exchange-rate movements introduce the only source of uncertainty in the model, thereby permitting consideration of exchange risk. The first model presented in this study isolates the effect of exchange risk on the optimal allocation of the capital asset budget. Subsequent models study the issues of the currency-denomination of debt, and of the foreign production and export decision.

2

Review of the Literature

Introduction

With the exception of natural resource development, direct foreign investment was not significant until after the second World War. The phenomenal
growth in the ownership of foreign-located income-producing assets began
in the mid-1950s, extending through the decade of the 1960s. This is coin-
cidental with the resumption of currency convertibility and a period of
relative exchange-rate stability.

The major currency realignments of the later 1960s and early 1970s were
the first to occur with substantial direct investments in place. This prompted
investigations of the effect of exchange-rate changes on the operations and
profitability of existing foreign investments. It has only been in the past
several years that research has begun to study the effect of exchange risk on
the operational and investment decisions of the multinational firm.

Existing Models of Exchange Risk and Direct Investment

Aliber (1970, 1971) was the first to present arguments relating exchange risk
and direct investment. Aliber suggested that the pattern of foreign direct
investment could be explained by differences in the cost of capital which are
created by exchange-risk premiums. Firms located in a preferred currency
country could borrow at lower interest rates or issue equity at higher
capitalization ratios because these liabilities are denominated in a currency
with lower perceived exchange risks.[1] This capital-cost advantage provides
source-country firms with the ability to compete in foreign markets.

Definitionally, firms obtaining funds in a preferred currency become
source-country firms. Firms which raise funds in a higher-risk currency must
pay an exchange-risk premium for these funds, effectively limiting their
ability to compete outside of the local market. Aliber's argument also
provides an explanation for the existence of "cross-hauling" (simultaneous
direct investment by firms in both countries). According to Aliber, host-

country firms are encouraged to invest in the source country to obtain earnings denominated in the lower-risk currency. These earnings assist in lowering the host-country firms' cost of capital.

An inconsistency arises in Aliber's argument when source-country firms with earnings denominated in the host-country currency continue to receive preferential treatment in the capital markets. Presumably, as the percentage of foreign-currency-denominated income rises, so should the firms' cost of capital, thereby removing its competitive advantage. Aliber resolves this inconsistency by arguing that multinational firms provide a diversification benefit to the investor which serves to negate the added exposure to risk, or as another possibility, investors may be ignorant as to the source of the firms' earnings.

Dufey (1972) discusses the potential impact of exchange-rate changes on *local-currency* costs and revenues. To quote:

> A fundamental point is that local currency revenue and cost streams will not follow the pattern projected before the devaluation. In fact, after the devaluation, these local currency flows will exhibit differences that are systematic and predictable as to direction. Therefore, a uniform, indiscriminate application of the devaluation percentage to the projected predevaluation flow gives an inaccurate picture (Dufey, 1972, p. 52)

Factors which influence local-currency revenues include the destination of production (export or local market), the source and degree of competition (domestic or foreign), and the effect of currency changes on real incomes. The factors cited as influencing local-currency costs include the proportion of imported materials used in production, the degree of competition among suppliers, and the amount of slack in the local economy. Dufey states that the net effect of these influences, in domestic currency terms, can only be determined on a case-by-case basis.

Heckerman (1972) defines the value of foreign operations as the present discounted value of a foreign income stream. By evaluating local currency flows in real terms, Heckerman found that fluctuations in the terms of trade could result in significant capital gains and losses.[2] Heckerman's results, while meaningful, were constrained by the assumption that real sales levels and the margin between revenues and costs are unaffected by fluctuations in the terms of trade.

Stevens (1972) uses an interesting approach in studying the investment and financing decisions of the multinational firm. Stevens accepts the Modigliani-Miller theorem which states that under certain restrictive conditions (such as the absence of taxes) the firms' financial decisions have no influence on its market value.[3] This permits Stevens to simplify the value maximization problem by separating the direct investment and financing decisions.

Stevens assumes that the firm is a value maximizer. The level of foreign investment (plant, equipment, current assets) is solved by setting the marginal revenue product of each asset equal to its shadow price.[4] The indeterminancy in the firms' financing policy is resolved by assuming that the firm minimizes exchange-rate losses on its borrowings while financing the level of real investment required to maximize the firms' market value. Implicitly, Stevens assumes that exchange risk is limited to the financial side of the firm and does not affect the return on the firms' real assets. This study assumes that exchange-rate changes can affect the return on real assets and should, therefore, be considered when real asset decisions are made.

Stevens is able to test the model empirically by further assuming that there is no correlation between exchange rates, and that the financing decision is reevaluated each year. Consistent with the Modigliani-Miller theorem, Stevens does not consider taxes, a factor which is critical in financing decisions.

Shapiro (1975) studies the effect of inflation and exchange-rate changes on the operations and value of the multinational firm. Shapiro, in agreement with Dufey (1972), recognizes that local currency costs and revenues are sensitive to the rate of exchange. This recognition leads Shapiro to conclude:

> ... The major factors affecting a multinational firms' exchange risk include the distribution of its sales between domestic and export markets, the amount of import competition it faces domestically, and the degree of substitutability between local and imported factors of production (Shapiro, 1975, p. 486).

Shapiro derives these results by including the exchange rate as an argument in the firms' local currency cost and revenue functions. The magnitude of the change in the firms' costs and revenue flows with respect to the change in the exchange rate depends on the source and degree of competition facing the firm. This study adopts a similar convention by including the exchange rate as an argument in the local-currency product price, and local-currency wage functions.[5]

Logue and Willett (1977) argue that international capital flows are stimulated by exchange-rate changes due to investor portfolio rebalancing. Logue and Willett reason that if investors' mean-variance expectations are unaffected by a currency realignment, the utility maximizing percentages of each assets' holding relative to the total portfolio will be left unaltered. Since the currency realignment alters the value of each asset in the portfolio, capital flows will be stimulated as investors readjust their portfolio holdings to reflect the unaltered optimal percentages. The authors argue that this effect may be applicable to both financial and real asset portfolios.

This study argues that changing exchange rates will in most instances cause real economic changes. These changes alter the risk-return attributes of the portfolios' assets, again changing investors' mean-variance expectations. In the Logue and Willett model, this would create a further stimulus for portfolio adjustments and the resulting capital flows.

Guy V. G. Stevens (1977) in a comment to the above-cited Logue and Willett paper, develops a model which indicates that a currency adjustment can produce virtually any result regarding the relative profitability of domestic versus foreign production. To quote:

> . . . depending on the alternative ways a devaluation of the dollar can affect the costs and revenues of diect investment, one can make a plausible theoretical case for *any* outcome: the devaluation may discourage U.S. direct investment abroad, encourage it or leave it unchanged. We can arrive at such differing conclusions because there are a number of different ways that devaluations can affect the revenues and costs of foreign subsidiaries (Stevens, 1977, p. 184).

Stevens shows that the effect of a devaluation on the profitability of foreign production depends on such considerations as the dollar (local currency) denominated content of the foreign (domestic) subsidiaries' cost function, the degree of substitutability of domestic and foreign production, and the slope of the revenue function. Direct foreign investment is influenced by changes in the profitability of foreign production in Steven's model.

Kohlhagen (1977a) in a comment on the Logue and Willett paper, presents a model which allows for domestic production and the exportation of output. Kohlhagen then investigates the effect of a devaluation on the relative profitability of domestic versus foreign production. Kohlhagen proceeds to argue that direct foreign investment is based on the profitability of foreign production *relative* to the profitability of domestic production (and exportation). Kohlhagen derives conclusions regarding the location of direct investment which support those of the Logue and Willett paper.

Kohlhagen (1977b), in a subsequent paper, further develops the model presented in Kohlhagen (1977a). Kohlhagen is able to show, under a very restrictive set of conditions, that devaluation of the domestic currency will unambiguously favor domestic production and export relative to direct foreign investment and foreign production.[6] Under less restrictive assumptions, Kohlhagen is able to state the conditions for which the relative profitability of domestic production is enhanced by a currency devaluation. Kohlhagen then presents empirical results.

Kohlhagen demonstrates that the relative profitability of domestic versus foreign production is influenced by movements in the exchange rate. Kohlhagen does not address the issue of *exchange risk*; rather, Kohlhagen studies how the *level of the exchange rate* influences profitability and the incentives for foreign direct investment relative to domestic production and exportation.

Many writers have used the Capital Asset Pricing Model (CAPM) to investigate the effect of exchange risk on economic behavior. Most attempts fail when the model is internationalized.[7] The CAPM postulates that the market price of an asset is determined by a risk-free rate of return, the market price of risk, and the covariance of the asset's return with the market return. The pricing relationship is described below:

$$E(\tilde{R}_i) = R_f + \beta Cov(\tilde{R}_i, \tilde{R}_m) \qquad\qquad 2.00$$

where $E(\tilde{R}_i)$ = expected return on risky asset (i)

$\quad\quad R_f$ = risk-free rate of return

$\quad\quad \tilde{R}_m$ = return on market portfolio

$\quad\quad \beta$ = market price of risk

Several difficulties arise when trying to "internationalize" the CAPM. Problems include the specification of an international risk-free rate of return (R_f), and in specifying an internationally consistent market price of risk (β). The existence of exchange risk may lead investors to favor assets denominated in the currency of their own consumption, thereby differentiating β's by currency area. Various constraints to the movement of capital may prevent international asset pricing equalization, also leading to capital-market segmentation by legal jurisdiction.[8]

Wuster (1978), in an unpublished doctoral dissertation, overcomes some of these difficulties by developing a "hybrid" model, an international capital asset pricing relationship *specific* to each domestic market. Firms are assumed to be value maximizers, and, according to Wuster, evaluate their international decisions relative to a domestic capital asset pricing relationship. Wuster argues that investors evaluate investment returns in the domestic currency (the currency of consumption) and with capital-market segmentation assumed, compare these investment returns to the domestic-market portfolio return.

According to Wuster's model, the foreign investment decision is specified as follows:

Invest if:

$$E(\tilde{R}_i) = E(\tilde{R}_i^e) + E(\tilde{\varepsilon}) \qquad\qquad 2.01$$
$$> R_f + \beta Cov(\tilde{R}_i^e, \tilde{R}_m) + \beta Cov(\tilde{\varepsilon}, \tilde{R}_m)$$

where $E(\tilde{R}_i^e)$ = expected return measured in foreign currency

$\quad\quad E(\tilde{\varepsilon})$ = expected rate of appreciation of foreign currency

Wuster is able to isolate the exchange-risk premium ($\beta\text{Cov}(\tilde{e}, \tilde{R}_m)$) by separating the return on a foreign asset into its nominal local-currency return ($\tilde{R}_i^e$) and an element representing the change in the rate of exchange ($\tilde{e}$). The problem with this approach is that it fails to consider "real" exchange risk, or the change in the nominal local-currency return ($\tilde{R}_i^e$) that results when the exchange rate changes. In other words, Wuster implicitly assumes that $\text{Cov}(\tilde{R}_i^e, \tilde{e}) = 0$, or to quote directly, "the dollar expected return from the investment is just the foreign currency expected return plus the anticipated appreciation of the foreign currency relative to the dollar" (Wuster, p. 20). This assumption precludes real economic effects (changes in sales levels, for example) from occurring when exchange rates change.

Mehra (1978) also uses a capital asset pricing model to investigate the effects of exchange risk on the financial and investment decisions of the multinational firm. Mehra's results include a term which recognizes the relationship between the exchange rate and local-currency asset returns. Therefore, all of the firms' decisions reflect an adjustment for real exchange risk. The difficulty with Mehra's approach is the assumption of perfectly integrated world capital markets. As a result, firms are instructed to evaluate financial and investment alternatives with reference to a world-market portfolio. Mehra's approach also requires the independent evaluation of the firms' financing and investment decisions. This is proper if the exchange-risk aspects of financial and real assets are independent. However, as this study demonstrates, the financing decision can alter the risk characteristics of foreign real assets. The interrelated risk relationship of real and financial assets requires their simultaneous consideration in the firms' decision process.

Calderon-Rossel (1978), in an unpublished doctoral dissertation, studied the effect of exchange-rate uncertainty on the sourcing and sales decisions of the multinational firm. The modeling procedure used in this study is similar to that employed by Calderon-Rossel, the maximization of a linear utility function with expected profits and the variance of profits being arguments of the utility function. Calderon-Rossel's specification of exchange risk, as with most other studies in this area, failed to consider the effect of exchange-rate changes on local-currency prices or costs. Exchange risk is limited to the random movement of the exchange rate. To quote:

> The fluctuation of the foreign exchange rate, the foreign exchange risk, is defined as the variance of the foreign exchange rate. In this basic sourcing portfolio model the only risk the firm faces is the foreign exchange risk (Calderon-Rossel, 1978, p. 30).

In the Calderon-Rossel model, the variance of profits is equal to the variance of the exchange rate multiplied by the square of net profits denominated in the foreign currency. This type of exchange risk could be hedged in the forward markets since the only source of uncertainty is the end-of-period exchange rate.

Calderon-Rossel later assumes that prices and exchange rates are correlated, but it is assumed that the firms' product price influences the exchange rate (rather than the reverse) through a purchasing-power-parity condition.

Hartman (1979) uses a portfolio model approach to study domestic investment, direct foreign investment, and foreign borrowing levels in the aggregate. Hartman assumes that individual investors are risk-averse, and the investor therefore requires that in the aggregate firms pursue policies consistent with investor risk-averse preferences. Risk arises from two inseparable sources in the model;[9] the imperfect correlation of returns among countries and the exchange risk arising from foreign-currency-denominated debt.

Hartman solves his model for portfolios (domestic investment, foreign investment, foreign borrowings) which lie on the risk-return efficiency frontier. He is then able to study how the optimal levels of the assets contained in the portfolio are influenced by changes in exogenous parameters. The parameters studied include the sensitivity of asset returns to exchange-rate movements (exposure to exchange risk), and the level of various forms of income taxation.

One result of interest to this study is Hartman's finding that borrowing is preferred at the location where assets are employed. This preference increases as the sensitivity of asset returns to currency movements increases.

Summary

This chapter has reviewed the current "state of the art" in models that relate exchange-risk considerations to direct investment decisions. Two broad avenues of thought exist. The first avenue limits exchange-risk considerations to the financial aspects of the firm. This narrow view does not address the difficulties which arise when relative prices or real sales levels change. No consideration is given to the possibility that real (exchange-rate adjusted) profitability may be affected by exchange-rate changes.

With this limited view, exchange risk can be protected against by fixing the end-of-period exchange rate through the use of the forward or futures market or by the use of various borrowing techniques. Exchange risk is considered to be neutralized and is therefore not a factor for consideration in the direct investment decisions of the firm.

The second avenue of thought recognizes that exchange-rate adjustments can influence real economic activity. With this understanding, exchange risk is "real" and cannot be simply hedged away. Various mechanisms can be invoked which fix the end of period exchange rate, but this does not address the economic problem; the sensitivity to exchange-rate adjustments of the end-of-period sales rate, local-currency product prices, or local-currency material prices (including wages).

Under these conditions, exchange risk is "real". The exposure cannot be hedged away, and therefore becomes an appropriate factor for consideration in the direct investment decisions of the firm. The next chapter identifies the impact that changing exchange rates have on the value and operations of the firm. This background provides an understanding of how the investment decision and the related financing and export decisions are influenced by exposure to exchange risk.

3

Exchange Risk

Introduction

Exchange risk emanates from the impact of changing exchange rates on the valuation and operations of the firm. If changing rates have no influence on the firms' operation or market value, then exchange rates are not a source of risk to the firm, or the firm is not considered to be exposed to exchange risk.

Foreign exchange risk, purely defined, is the additional riskiness in financial outcomes that results when economic activity is conducted in markets where the currency of determination differs from that of the home market.[1] The currency of determination is the currency that ultimately influences transaction prices, and the quantities bought and sold. This may differ from the currency of denomination, or the currency used to settle transactions. Exposure to exchange risk depends on the individual firm's type of operation, its input and output markets, and its financial structure.

Exchange risk can be separated into two broad classifications, "accounting risk" and "economic risk." Accounting risk pertains to the impact of exchange-rate changes on the balance sheet and contractual flows of the firm. The value of stocks and flows denominated in foreign currencies is subject to change in their domestic-currency value as the prevailing rate of exchange changes. Economic risk or economic exposure is a term used for changes in the domestic value of non-contractual local currency flows. Economic exposure is the risk that the domestic value of the firms' cash flow may fluctuate with changes in the rate of exchange.

Beyond the horizon of current production, revenues and variable costs of the firm are typcially not under contract. A change in the prevailing rate of exchange can alter the domestic-currency value of these flows if the change is not fully reflected in adjustments in local-currency prices or if quantity adjustments result.

The various forms of exchange risk have different implications for the firm. Accounting risk presents operational problems which can be covered at an implicit or explicit cost to the firm. Economic risk cannot be covered, although it may be reduced through diversification. As a consequence, economic exposure is a factor for consideration in the investment decision of the firm. The discussion that follows briefly identifies each form of exchange risk and highlights its relevance to the firm's investment decision.

Accounting Risk

Under the title of accounting risk are two forms of risk to consider: translation risk and transaction risk.

Translation Risk

Prindl (1976, p. 2) offers a concise perspective on accounting risk:

> 'Accounting risk' relates to the necessity to value disparate assets, liabilities and income items in terms of a single currency. The risk element is that the publicly stated value of the company's assets, equity, and income may be adversely affected by the movement of currencies in which it has dealings.

This definition of accounting risk refers to the effect of exchange-rate changes on balance-sheet items. More precisely, this form of accounting risk is usually termed "translation risk."

Until recently, the Financial Accounting Standards Board Ruling No. 8 (issued in October 1975) governed multinational accounting procedures pertaining to foreign-currency transactions and foreign-currency financial statements.[2] The FASB ruling was intended to develop a common and coherent accounting standard for use by U.S.-based multinationals. The FASB No. 8 standard succeeded in establishing a set of common procedures; unfortunately, however, in the process all multinationals became subject to the same set of distortions created by its adoption.

FASB No. 8 contained two requirements: the method or procedure to be used in translation, and the necessity of reporting translation gains or losses as income. Aggarwal (1978, p. 200) summarizes these requirements:

> FASB No. 8 is based on the temporal principle which states that cash, receivables, and payables measured at amounts promised should be translated at the exchange rate in effect at the balance-sheet date, while assets and liabilities measured at money prices should be translated at the foreign exchange rate in effect at the dates to which the money prices pertain. Besides recommending the translation rates to be used, FASB No. 8, in addition, recommends that all translation-related losses and gains be fully recognized as part of net income in each quarter.

Foreign-currency-denominated assets and liabilities translated each accounting period at historical exchange rates were not exposed to varia-tions in the exchange rate.[3] Fixed assets were typically translated at historical exchange rates and therefore were not considered to be exposed. Most other assets and virtually all liabilities were periodically translated at current rates and were subject to changes in value which reflected changes in the rate of exchange.

As exchange rates fluctuated, distortions began to appear in the consoli-dated quarterly financial statements of most multinationals. A major problem was created by the different treatment afforded to long-term debt and fixed assets. Long-term debt was translated at the current exchange rate, whereas fixed assets were translated at historical rates. The translated value of foreign debt would change each quarter, but its offset on the balance sheet, fixed assets, would not be adjusted. To compound the problem, these distortions were reported each quarter with other sources of income (or losses). Another problem developed when inventories were translated at historical rates, while the revenue from sales (which includes goods sold from inventory) was translated at current rates.

Translation gains and losses or the change in stated values which result from changes in exchange rates are considered by most to have no direct effect on the operations of the firm. These gains and losses are accounting artifacts and do not affect actual foreign-currency revenues or costs. Ian Giddy (1977, p. 31), a proponent of this view, wrote:

> . . . the shareholder might care only about balance sheet (accounting) gains and losses. If that is the case, as some in this field appear to believe, then the corporate treasurer should perhaps be concerned with matching assets defined by accounting rules as exposed with liabilities defined as exposed rather than with real (cash flow) exposure. Fortunately, however, a large body of evidence on stock price behavior supports the idea that the market can distinguish real from purely accounting effects on reported income. Changes in accounting methods do not appear to affect stock prices. Concern with balance sheet exposure, therefore, probably does not serve the shareholder's interests.

Theory aside, the magnitude of the quarterly swings in reported income caused by translation gains and losses prompted many corporations to use various techniques to manage their exposure to translation risk. In Decem-ber of 1981, the Financial Accounting Standards Board issued Statement No. 52, "Foreign Currency Translation" as a replacement for FASB State-ment No. 8.[4] FASB 52 permits companies to measure the performance of foreign operations in the "functional" currency of the local operation. Translation of all functional currency assets and liabilities is to be conducted at the current rate of exchange. This solves the measurement problems created by FASB No. 8 which translated balance sheet entries at different rates. FASB Statement No. 52 requires all assets and liabilities to be translated at the same rate. Under FASB No. 52, the only exposure is the translated value of the net worth of the foreign operation.

The new ruling, to be adopted by companies by 1983, also relieves the burden placed on the bottom line. Translation adjustments no longer have to be included with reported quarterly income. Rather, any adjustments to be made are included in shareholders' equity. FASB No. 52 appears to be a significant improvement over its predecessor. If, however, companies find that the exposure to shareholder equity results in unacceptable swings, it is likely that companies will adopt steps to hedge against this new accounting exposure.

Transaction Risk

Transaction risk exists when the currency of denomination in a transaction is foreign to one or both of the transactors. Transaction risk arises because of the time gap between the date when a transaction is initiated and the date when payment is made (usually on completion of the transaction). During that time the exchange rate may change with the party converting foreign exchange into domestic currency being subject to windfall gains or losses. Transaction risk exists in both trade and financial asset transactions.

Transaction risk can result in real monetary gains or losses for the firm. Hedging with forward exchange contracts and the leading and lagging of payments are techniques commonly used to protect against transaction risk. These techniques reduce exposure to exchange risk but involve additional expense. Some writers suggest that use of these hedging techniques may not be in the better interests of the firm. These beliefs are based on the premise that foreign-exchange markets are efficient, and therefore the forward exchange rate provides an unbiased estimate of the future spot rate. If this is the case, on average the forward rate will equal the future spot rate. As a result, firms are paying an insurance premium (in the case of hedging costs) to insure an outcome that they would receive on average without paying the insurance premium.

The argument against consistently hedging transaction risk succeeds if certain conditions are met. Foremost, the foreign-exchange markets must be efficient such that the forward exchange rate reflects all available market information. If this condition is not met, the forward rate would be a biased predictor of the future spot rates. Therefore, a consistently unhedged position would result in systematic gains or losses over long periods of time.

The pricing of risk premiums[5] in the spot or forward markets also would result in a consistent divergence between forward rates and future spot rates, even when the markets are considered to be efficient. In an efficient market, the firm would not benefit or be penalized in holding exposed positions unless the firms' internal price of risk differs from the market price of risk. Under such conditions, the firm would benefit in covering its exposure if its internal price is above the market price of risk, or in other words, the firm finds that the "insurance premium" is cheap relative to what it is willing to pay. In the reverse situation, the firm would benefit in remaining exposed if the pricing relationship is reversed.

Another prerequisite for limiting hedging practices is for the firm to be engaged in frequent transactions of roughly similar value to insure the law of averages (or law of large numbers) will hold. The firm engaged in infrequent transactions will find each transaction exposed to exchange risk, but will not have sufficient transaction to allow for the averaging process to insure the desired results.

Long-term foreign-currency-denominated debt also places the firm at risk unless appropriately hedged. A foreign-currency loan could result in real monetary gains or losses if exchange rates change in an unanticipated fashion.

In all cases, transaction exposure can be readily identified by the firm and fully hedged (at a cost) if desired.[6] Exposure to transaction risk is an *operational decision* of the firm based on expected returns, hedging costs, and attitudes toward risk. As such, transaction exposure is not a relevant consideration in the *investment decision* of the firm.

Economic Risk[7]

Economic exposure or economic risk refers to the uncertain influence changing exchange rates may have on the revenue and cost structure of the firm. The cost of foreign production may change in response to exchange-rate changes because inputs are imported or, if locally acquired, face international competition. Revenues may change as a result of changing rates of exchange because output is destined for the export market or, if sold locally, may face import competition. Local production fully insulated from the world marketplace (on the input and output level) may still be exposed to exchange risk because of the income effect of exchange-rate changes.

Economic exposure arises because the firm cannot contractually fix over sufficiently long periods of time, its sales level, price levels, or cost of inputs. These values are subject to change as the exchange-rate changes. As a result, the local-currency profit margin of the firm becomes sensitive to exchange-rate movements. The discussion that follows describes the factors which give rise to economic exposure.[8]

Deviations from Purchasing Power Parity (PPP)

A deviation from PPP implies that the change in exchange rates is not fully reflected in price-level changes.[9] For example, if a bottle of French wine sells for 20 francs, and the rate of exchange is four francs to the dollar, the bottle will sell for five dollars. A 25 percent devaluation (or depreciation) of the franc, coupled with a 25 percent increase in the local price of the wine leaves the dollar price of the wine unchanged, or purchasing power parity is maintained. (Twenty-five francs at five francs to the dollar equals the same five-dollar price for the bottle of wine.) If the percentage change in the exchange rate does not match the percentage change in local prices, the translated price will change, and the purchasing power of the currencies will have been altered.[10]

Assuming production levels and local-currency profit margins remain fixed, the translated value of profits and net worth of the subsidiary will be altered by the percentage deviation from PPP. In essence, this is comparable to "real" translation risk, the risk that the real translated value of the subsidiary will change in response to exchange-rate changes. Figures 1 and 2 provide an example.

Figure 1. Economic Risk When Purchasing Power Parity Holds

Pre-Devaluation
(Local Price =20ff   4ff =$1)

Unit Sales	Gross Income	Profit @ 10%	Profits in $
1,000	20,000ff	2,000ff	$500

Post-Devaluation
(Local Price =25ff   5ff =$1)

Unit Sales	Gross Income	Profit @ 10%	Profits in $
1,000	25,000ff	2,500ff	$500

Figure 2. Economic Risk and Deviations from Purchasing Power Parity

Pre-Devaluation
(Local Price =20ff   4ff=$1)

Unit Sales	Gross Income	Profit @ 10%	Profits in $
1,000	20,000ff	2,000ff	$500

Post-Devaluation
(Local Price =22ff   5ff=$1)

Unit Sales	Gross Income	Profit @ 10%	Profits in $
1,000	22,000ff	2,200ff	$440

In the extreme situation, if all local-currency costs, selling prices, and sales quantities are contractually fixed, the level of *local-currency* profits is insulated from exchange-rate adjustments. Local-currency profits will not vary with the rate of exchange. The problem is, however, that the *translated value* of the local-currency profits will vary directly with the percentage change in the exchange rate. As unlikely as this situation is, the risk this presents can be protected against.

Under this set of conditions, the subsidiary could borrow in the local capital market the local-currency equivalent of the present value of expected future profits. This sum is then converted to domestic currency and reinvested. This permits the parent company to realize the domestic-currency value of the subsidiary's future profit stream without concern for future currency movements. The local-currency profit flow of the subsidiary is then used to amortize the loan.

This procedure is only successful if all of these flows are contractually fixed. A change in prices or quantities would alter the relationship between the local-currency profit flow and the repayment of local-currency debt.

A more likely condition is for deviations from PPP to change the competitive position of the tradable goods sector relative to world markets and the local non-tradable goods sector. A depreciation will increase factor employment, production, and local prices in the tradable goods sector. A currency appreciation will have a depressing effect on employment, production, and prices. The impact on the local-currency profits of the firm depends on the source and degree of competition in the firm's input and output markets.

Inputs, including labor and raw materials, can be imported or sourced domestically. If imported, these inputs would fully reflect the change in exchange rates. The local-currency cost of locally-sourced inputs reflects changes in exchange rates to the extent that the local markets face import competition. The change in input costs can range from nil (fully isolated from import competition) to the full extent of the exchange-rate change (direct import competition). (See figure 3.)

Output directed towards the export market or directly facing import competition will change in price in relation to the change in currency values. The local-currency price of production in the non-tradable goods sector is insulated from exchange-rate changes. Production facing indirect import competition will be partially affected by currency-price movements. (See figure 4). Table 1 summarizes these effects on the profit margin of the local subsidiary using a local-currency depreciation as an example.

In seven of nine cases, local-currency profit margins per unit of output are altered after a local-currency depreciation. (The direction of change is reversed for an appreciation.) The duration of these changes may be

Figure 3. Foreign Output Prices, Exchange Rates and the Degree of
        Competition from World Markets

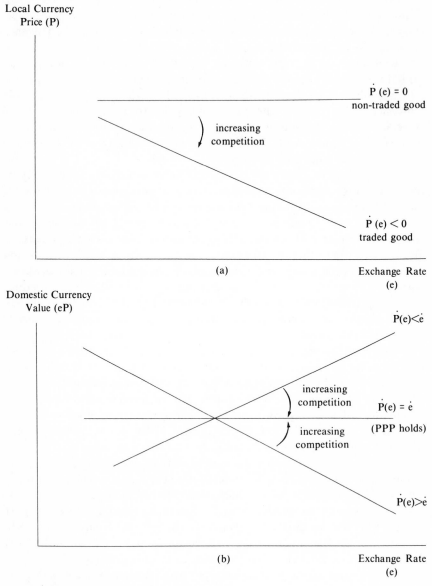

Local Currency
   Price (P)

$\dot{P}$ (e) = 0
non-traded good

increasing
competition

$\dot{P}$ (e) < 0
traded good

(a)   Exchange Rate
                                              (e)

Domestic Currency
   Value (eP)

$\dot{P}$(e)<$\dot{e}$

increasing
competition

$\dot{P}$(e) = $\dot{e}$

(PPP holds)

increasing
competition

$\dot{P}$(e)>$\dot{e}$

(b)   Exchange Rate
                                              (e)

Note: $\dot{P}$ indicates percent change in P or $\Delta P/P$
       $\dot{e}$ indicates percent change in e or $\Delta P/e$

Figure 4. Foreign Wage Costs, Exchange Rates and the Degree of
Competition from World Markets

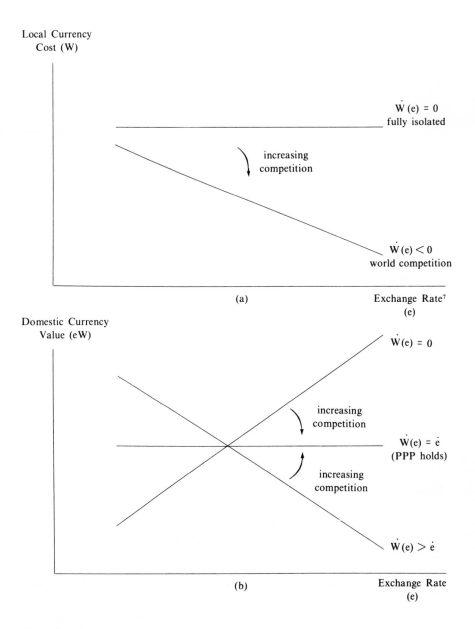

Note: $\dot{w}$ indicates percent change in w or $\Delta w/w$

Table 1. Impact of Local-Currency Depreciation on Local-Currency Profit
Margins (Output Fixed)

Market for Inputs	World	Market for Output Domestic with Import Comp.	Domestic Insulated
World	0	$\leqslant 0$	< 0
Domestic with Import Comp.	$\geqslant 0$	$\lesseqgtr 0$	$\leqslant 0$
Domestic Insulated	> 0	$\geqslant 0$	0

temporary or long-term, depending on the causes and result of the exchange-rate change. The exposure of local-currency profit flows should be a factor of consideration in the firm's investment decision.

Unanticipated Price Level Adjustments

Local inflation and exchange-rate adjustments affect local price levels. When these changes are unanticipated, they will not be accurately reflected in the terms of local-currency contracts. Unanticipated price-level adjustments affect local-currency profit margins to the extent that revenues and costs are not equally fixed in contract terms (e.g., selling prices but not costs may be contractually fixed).

   With the exception of tax depreciation schedules, the firm has operational control over the establishment of contracts. Unfortunatley, if the firm attempts to reduce exchange risk by shortening or eliminating contracts, it increases other operating risks by increasing the uncertainty of future costs and revenue flows.

Relative Price Effects

Although PPP may hold, exchange-rate changes can induce relative price changes due to uneven adjustments within the local economy. Purchasing power parity implies that a unit of currency can command control over an equivalent amount of resources before and after a currency adjustment. This may hold true for a weighted basket of goods, while not holding true for particular commodities within the basket. The potential problem raised here is that the price level (which is a weighted average of individual prices) may remain constant whereas particular prices which are components of the price level may change. Exchange rates directly influence goods which are tradable, while only indirectly affecting the prices of non-tradable goods.

Exchange-rate induced relative-price adjustments can significantly alter local-currency profit margins. These margins adjust depending on the nature of competition in the subsidiary's input and output markets.

Relative price changes also induce substitution effects which alter the demand for output. These effects cannot be predicted a priori without knowledge of the price elasticity of substitution and the effect of exchange-rate change on the pricing of substitutes.

Relative price changes can alter per-unit local-currency profit margins and with substitution effects, can alter the demand for output. The firm has limited operational control over these changes and as a result profit flows are exposed to risk. This form of exposure should be a matter of consideration in the firm's investment analysis.

Real Income Effect

A change in the real rate of exchange alters real income in the local economy. Workers employed in the tradable goods sectors may find their wage bargaining power influenced by the changing competitive position of the products they produce. Various forms of wealth within the country may also be sensitive to exchange rates, such as the holdings of foreign assets and foreign liabilities.

Firms selling income-sensitive products in the local market may find demand influenced by the exchange-rate change. Consideration of income effects in the investment decision should depend on the income sensitivity of the product markets.

Summary

Foreign direct investment is exposed to several forms of risk as exchange rates change.[11] Economic risk cannot be clearly isolated or managed, although opportunities may exist to minimize risk through investment diversification.

The firm cannot fully protect against economic risk. Accordingly, this form of exposure needs to be considered in the investment decision of the firm. The following chapter presents a theoretical model which permits the incorporation of economic exchange risk into the investment decision of the firm.

4

Exchange Risk and the
Investment Decision

Introduction

This chapter presents a theoretical model of the firm operating in two
markets. The model is used to explore how the firm reacts to various changes
in the economic environment. The changes in the environment are induced
by changes in the rate of exchange. The responses that are studied are the
optimal level of capital investment in the two markets, the optimal proportion of total debt to be denominated in the foreign currency, and the optimal
production and sales levels in each market. The direct investment decision is
reviewed in this chapter. Chapter 5 investigates the debt-denomination
question. The production and sales decisions are highlighted in chapter 6.

Theoretical Model

Consider a two-country world. Country 1, the source country and location
of the domestic market, is where management and the firm's shareholders
reside. Transactions, financial results, and consumption are measured in the
domestic currency. Initially assume that Country 2, the host country and
location of the foreign or local market, is small relative to the size of Country
1.[1] Investment in the domestic market is subject to normal business risks but
is not subject to exchange risk. Direct investment in Country 2 is subject to
normal business risks, political or country risks, and exchange risk. Since we
are concerned with the impact of exchange risk on direct investment, other
forms of risk are assumed away. For purposes of this analysis, business and
political risks can be considered as equivalent for all investments and
therefore not a distinguishing factor for consideration.

The domestic and foreign markets are assumed to be competitive. The
firm sells its output in the market where it is produced. Output (Q) is a
function of two inputs, physical capital (K) and labor (L).[2] Labor can be

considered as a proxy for all forms of variable inputs to the production process including, for example, raw materials, intermediate products, and labor itself. In essence, labor is used as a "catch-all" to represent the non-capital inputs used in production.

In this chapter, we are primarily concerned with investment, or the commitment of new capital to production. The level of capital employed at any point in time represents the summation of investments made in prior years.[3] Existing capital is assumed to be immobile; it cannot be redeployed and therefore represents a "sunk" or fixed cost. A sunk or fixed cost is not considered in the value maximization problem since it does not influence decisions on the margin, such as decisions relating to the commitment of new capital.

Existing capital appears in the production function, since the level of output depends on the previously existing level of capital investment (K), the level of new investment (I), and the level of labor employment (L). The production function is written as $Q_i = F_i(K_i + I_i, L_i)$. The subscript is used to denote the location of activity. For newly established investment projects, $K_i = 0$. The production function summarizes the technological relationship that exists between the level of inputs (K, I, L) and the level of output (Q). It is assumed that the firm is faced with an upward sloped supply curve for new capital (investment). As the firm attempts to increase its investment levels (I) in the short run, it finds that r, the per-unit cost of capital, rises. (See figure 5.) This is stated as follows:[4]

$$r = r(I) = r(\Sigma I_i)$$

with $r' = dr/dI > 0$ and $r'' = 0$.

The subscripts refer to the location where the new capital is employed. This assumption indicates the constrained access that firms have to new capital, thereby requiring internal projects to compete against each other for a share of the capital budget.[5]

There are two equally plausible justifications for using such an assumption. On the financial side, the firm may find that in the short run lenders or investors become increasingly reluctant to supply the firm with new funds as the firms' investment requirements rise. These investors or lenders may perceive that risks increase as the firms' rate of expansion rises (new investment relative to the existing capital base). Accordingly, lenders would require a higher interest rate and investors pay a lower capitalization rate as the firm increases its investment levels in the short run.

Considering real assets, the firm may experience increasing costs of adjustment as its rate of physical expansion rises. As the firm tries to expand

Figure 5. Short-Run Supply Curve for New Capital

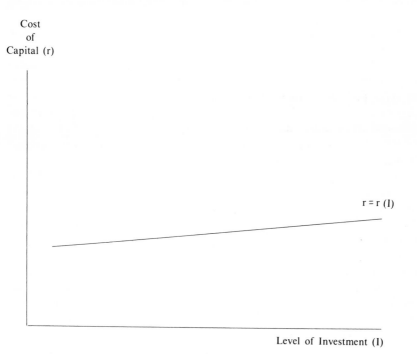

Cost
of
Capital (r)

$r = r (I)$

Level of Investment (I)

its physical capacity too rapidly, it experiences difficulties with untrained labor, inexperienced new management, poorly developed raw material sources, and so on. Under such conditions, the firm would find each unit of new capital being less productive (with the capital-labor ratio held constant). Viewed differently, the firm finds that the effective cost of capital per unit of output rises as the rate of physical expansion increases.

The firm finds the local currency price of output, P_2, and the local currency price of labor inputs, W_2, sensitive to the rate of exchange, e. With e defined as domestic currency (\$) per unit of foreign currency (£), we can state the following:[6]

$$e = \$/£$$

$$P_2 = P_2(e) \qquad \frac{dP_2(e)}{de} = P_2'(e) \leqslant 0$$

$$W_2 = W_2(e) \qquad \frac{dW'_2(e)}{de} = W_2'(e) \leqslant 0$$

As e rises, the foreign currency is appreciating in value relative to the domestic currency (more $ per £), thereby exerting downward pressure on the local currency prices of output and inputs.

Of concern to management is the domestic currency value of these flows, $eP_2(e)$ and $eW_2(e)$. When PPP holds and there are no relative price or income effects, exchange-rate changes will be identically offset by changes in local-currency prices. (Refer to discussion on pages 9–10.) Therefore, $eP_2(e)$ and $eW_2(e)$ can be treated as constants with the same degree of certainty as prices and wages in the domestic market. However, if any of these conditions are not satisfied (PPP, no relative price effects, no income effects), $eP_2(e)$ and $eW_2(e)$ become uncertain. This indicates that cash flow from foreign operations is subject to variation when exchange rates change. The uncertain nature of $eW_2(e)$ and $eP_2(e)$ introduces exchange risk into the model.

Decisions are influenced by the random nature of prices, costs, and profits because of an assumed aversion to risk. Risk-averse behavior can be justified by one of several arguments.[7] An "entrepreneurial model" assumes the firm is operated by a single owner or individual with a controlling interest in the firm. Operating and investment decisions are consistent with the entrepreneur's risk-averse preferences.

Alternatively, one can stipulate that ownership is separated from control with the structure of management compensation guiding managers' behavior in a risk-averse manner. Higher profits ensure continued employment; lower profits lead to termination.

As discussed previously, imperfect international capital markets can also be used to justify risk-averse firm behavior. If returns are not perfectly correlated internationally, a mean-variance efficient portfolio will contain foreign assets. Impediments that prevent portfolio diversification at the investor level can be effectively overcome by the resources of larger firms. As a result, the objectives of individual investors are satisfied by the purchase of shares in multinational firms which exhibit "risk-averse behavior."

The model presented here posits the investment decision of the firm as one of selecting the appropriate portfolio of real assets. The firm (its owner or manager) is risk averse and prefers: portfolios with the lowest risk among portfolios of equivalent expected return; and portfolios with the highest expected return among portfolios of equivalent risk. Since exchange risk is the only source of uncertainty in this model, the variance of profits can be considered a proxy for exchange risk.

This formulation is the standard Markowitz/Tobin prescription for portfolio selection. A utility function is used to rank the different portfolios. The portfolios in this particular specification contain various combinations of domestic and foreign real assets. The higher the expected return from a portfolio, the higher is the "utility" of the portfolio. Conversely, the higher the risk (the variance of expected returns) of the portfolio, the lower is the portfolio's "utility". The investor is then left with the task of evaluating the portfolios' risk/return attributes, ranking the portfolio according to a utility measure, and selecting the portfolio with the highest utility.[8]

The profits of the firm are a composite of returns from different investments. In the two-country case, one investment is domestic, the other foreign. The foreign investment is denominated in the foreign currency and its cash flow is sensitive to changing exchange rates. The model is summarized by the following equation system:*

Market 1

$$\pi_1 = P_1 Q_1(K_1 + I_1, L_1) - W_1 L_1 - r(I)I_1 \tag{4.00}$$

$$E(\pi_1) \equiv \bar{\pi}_1 = \pi_1 \tag{4.01}$$

$$\text{Var}(\bar{\pi}_1) \equiv \sigma^2_{\pi_1} = 0 \tag{4.02}$$

Market 2

$$\tilde{\pi}_2 = \tilde{e}\tilde{P}_2(e)Q_2(K_2 + I_2, L_2) - \tilde{e}\tilde{W}_2 L_2 - r(I)I_2 \tag{4.03}$$

$$E(\tilde{\pi}_2) \equiv \bar{\pi}_2 = \overline{eP}_2(e)Q_2(K_2 + I_2, L_2) - \overline{eW}_2 L_2 - r(I)I_2 \tag{4.04}$$

$$\text{Var}(\tilde{\pi}_2) \equiv \sigma^2_{\pi_2} = Q_2^2(K_2 + I_2, L_2)\,\sigma^2_{ep} + L_2^2\sigma^2_{ew} \tag{4.05}$$

$$- 2Q_2(K_2 + I_2, L_2)L_2\sigma^2_{epew}$$

---

*In these equations the following symbols are used:

π = profits
$E(x)$ = Expected or Mean Value of x
$\text{Var}(x)$ = Variance of x

A tilde ($\tilde{\ }$) indicates a random variable. A bar ($\bar{\ }$) indicates an expected value with $E(eP_2(e)) = \overline{eP}_2(e) \neq \bar{e} \cdot \bar{P}_2(e)$. Also note that $I = I_1 + I_2$, σ^2_{epew} denotes the covariance between $eP_2(e)$ and $eW_2(e)$; σ^2_{ep} denotes the variance of $eP_2(e)$; and σ^2_{ew} represents the variance of $eW_2(e)$.

Combining markets,

$$\bar{\pi} \equiv \bar{\pi}_1 + \bar{\pi}_2 = P_1 Q_1(K_1+I_1,L_1) \qquad\qquad 4.06$$

$$+ \ \overline{eP_2(e)} Q_2(K_2+I_2,L_2) \ -W_1 L_1$$

$$- \ \overline{eW_2(e)} L_2 \ -r(I)I$$

$$\sigma_\pi^2 = Q_2^2(K_2+I_2,L_2) \ \sigma_{ep}^2 +L_2^2 \sigma_{ew}^2 \qquad\qquad 4.07$$

$$- \ 2Q_2(K_2+I_2,L_2)L_2\sigma_{epew}^2$$

The variance is a measure of the "volatility" or instability of a particular variable. Mathematically it is the average of the squared deviations from the mean of a distribution; it is a measure of the dispersion of observed values around the average (expected) value. As the variance of a variable increases, we can expect the actual values of the variable to be further and further away from the expected value of the variable. If the variance of the profit flow is small, management should pay little attention to exchange risk since the risk we are concerned with (the variance of the profit flow) is small. A large variance of profits would result in the opposite conclusion being reached.

The covariance of two variables is a measure of the tendency of the variables in question to react in a consistent manner to a change in a third (independent) variable. If both variables respond in a very similar fashion, then the covariance is large in magnitude. The sign of the covariance is positive if the dependent variables change in the same direction, and is negative if the variables change in opposite directions. If local wages and local prices both increase when the local currency depreciates, the covariance of local wages with local prices will be large and positive. If local wages increase and local prices fall, the covariance will be large and negative. To the extent one of the variables does not repond to changes in the exchange rate, the covariance will be close to zero in value.[9]

Equation 4.00 is the profit function for the domestic market.[10] Total revenue is given by P_1Q_1, with W_1L_1 representing the wage bill for the production of Q_1, and rI_1 representing the cost of employing new capital, I_1.[11] Equation 4.01 states that the expected value of the profit flow, $E(\pi_1)$ is equal to π_1, since all terms in 4.00 are non-stochastic. As equation 4.02 indicates, the variance of a non-stochastic variable (π_1) is zero.

Equation 4.03 is the profit equation for the foreign market. Revenues are equal to the level of production, Q_2, times the local-currency selling price, P_2, times the rate of exchange, e. All local-currency values are converted to domestic-currency equivalents for decision-making purposes. The wage bill is represented by the level of labor inputs, L_2, times the local wage rate, W_2, times the rate of exchange. The cost of newly employed capital is given by rl_2.

The cost of investment in the second market (rl_2) is not affected by movements of the exchange rate. In this model, it is implicitly assumed that new capital is raised in the domestic market. Therefore, the cost of capital, r, is invariant with respect to the exchange rate. This restriction is dropped in the next chapter.

Profits in the second market are uncertain, given the random nature of e, $P_2(e)$, and $W_2(e)$. Equation 4.04 gives the expected domestic-currency value of the profit flow. The variance term (4.05) indicates that the level of risk associated with activity in the second market is positively related to the level of production, the level of labor usage, and the variances of the translated price, eP_2, and the translated wage, eW_2. The variance of profits is reduced to the extent that eP_2 and eW_2 are positively correlated ($\sigma^2_{epew} > 0$). As these values move in the same direction, the profit flow becomes increasingly insulated from exchange-rate movements. If these values are uncorrelated, or move in opposite directions, then profits become very sensitive to exchange-rate changes.

Equation 4.06 represents the expected profit level for the firm, which is obtained by summing expected profits from both markets (equation 4.01 and 4.04). The variance term in equation 4.07 covers all of the firms' operations. The variance is fully related to operations in the foreign market since domestic operations are considered risk-free.

Assuming a utility function of the form $E(u(\pi)) = \bar{\pi} - b\sigma^2_\pi$, the problem becomes one of selecting the input levels of L_1, I_1, L_2, I_2 which maximize the value of the unconstrained utility function. The value of b measures the marginal disutility of increased risk relative to the marginal utility of an increased unit of expected profit, and can be considered as a measure of the degree of risk aversion.[12] Stated differently, b is a measure of the decision makers' willingness to sacrifice return in order to reduce risk. A large value of b indicates conservative or risk-averse preferences.

The profit and variance relationships described in equations 4.00 through 4.07 are incorporated into the utility function. The resultant decision model is stated in 4.08 below:[13]

Maximize $E(U(\pi)) = \bar{\pi} - b\sigma^2_\pi$

L_1, I_1, L_2, I_2

$$= P_1Q_1(K_1+I_1,L_1) +e\overline{P}_2Q_2(K_2+I_2,L_2) -W_1L_1 \qquad 4.08$$

$$- e\overline{W}_2L_2 -r(I)I -b[Q_2^2(K_2+I_2,L_2)\sigma_{ep}^2 +L_2^2\sigma_{ew}^2$$

$$- 2Q_2(K_2+I_2,L_2)L_2\sigma_{epew}^2]$$

The task is to find the values of the four input stocks (L_1,I_1,L_2,I_2) which maximize the expected value of the utility function. Different input levels result in different levels of production. This influences costs, revenues, and exchange risk. The objective is to select the level of the inputs which produce an expected profit level and risk level (the variance of profits) which then, in turn, yields the maximum level of utility to the decision maker. Guidance in selecting the optimum input levels is given by the first-order conditions of the model. These conditions (which follow) must be satisfied to ensure that the utility maximizing decision has been reached.[14]

$$P_1Q_{L_1} -W_1 = 0 \qquad 4.09$$

$$P_1Q_{I_1} -r -r'I = 0 \qquad 4.10$$

$$e\overline{P}_2Q_{L_2} -e\overline{W}_2 -b[2Q_2Q_{L_2}\sigma_{ep}^2 +2L_2\sigma_{ew}^2 \qquad 4.11$$
$$-2Q_2\sigma_{epew}^2 -2L_2Q_{L_2}\sigma_{epew}^2] = 0$$

$$e\overline{P}_2Q_{I_2} -r -r'I -b[2Q_2Q_{I_2}\sigma_{ep}^2 \qquad 4.12$$
$$-2L_2Q_{I_2}\sigma_{epew}^2] = 0$$

Note that Q_{L_1}, Q_{I_1}, Q_{L_2}, Q_{I_2} represent the marginal products with respect to the subscripted inputs.

Interpretation of First-Order Conditions

Equation 4.09 states that in equilibrium, domestic labor (L_1) should be hired to the point where the marginal revenue product of labor $(P_1Q_{L_1})$ is equal to its marginal costs (W_1). Equation 4.10 states that the marginal revenue product of new capital employed in the domestic market $(P_1Q_{I_1})$ should equal its marginal cost $(r + r'I)$. It is worth noting that the marginal cost of capital investment is a function of the level of new investment employed firm-wide.

Equations 4.11 and 4.12 reflect the notion that utilization of L_2 and I_2 adds risk to the real asset portfolio. The addition of risk requires foreign projects to earn excess returns; i.e., in equilibrium, marginal revenue products exceed marginal costs. Equation 4.11 requires that the expected excess of the marginal revenue product of labor over its marginal cost $(eP_2Q_{L_2} - eW_2)$ be set equal to b times the marginal increase in the variance of profits due to an increase in labor usage $(b[2Q_2Q_{L_2}\sigma^2_{ep} + 2L_2\sigma^2_{ew} - 2Q_2\sigma^2_{epew} - 2L_2Q_{L_2}\sigma^2_{epew}])$. The excess of marginal revenue over marginal cost is the payment required to compensate for risk: it is the "risk-premium".

Equation 4.12 states a similar condition for foreign investment (I_2); in equilibrium, the expected excess of the marginal revenue product of capital over its marginal cost $(e\overline{P}_2Q_{I_2} - r - r'I)$ be set equal to b times the marginal increase in the variance of profits due to an increase in foreign investment $(b[2Q_2Q_{I_2}\sigma^2_{ep} - 2L_2Q_{I_2}\sigma^2_{epew}])$.

Specification of the production functions $Q_1(K_1+I_1,L_1)$ and $Q_2(K_2+I_2,L_2)$ allows equations 4.09 through 4.12 to be solved for the equilibrium values of I_1, I_2, L_1, and L_2. These values are substituted into equations 4.00 and 4.01 to solve for the utility maximizing levels of $\overline{\pi}$ and σ^2_π. These values are then used to solve equation 4.08 for the expected utility of profit. Parametric solutions (not shown here) result.[15]

Comparative Static Analysis

Of greater interest is how the optimal levels of input usage change in response to changes in the operating environment. Comparative-static derivatives were developed to demonstrate the direction of change in the endogenous variables in response to changes in the exogenous variables.[16]

The exogenous variables summarize the conditions of the operating environment, and are beyond the control of the firm. These variables include covariance measures of local prices and local wages. The endogenous variables are the measure that are under the firms' control. These variables include the levels of domestic and foreign capital investment, and the levels of domestic and foreign labor employment.

The signs of the comparative-static derivatives indicate how the firm should respond to changes in the operating environment in order to achieve the "optimal" or utility-maximizing portfolio. For example, an increase in domestic selling prices (P_1) indicates that the firm should increase its domestic investment and labor employment levels. In response to the same change, the firm should also reduce the levels of foreign investment and foreign labor employment. These conditions are summarized in table 2.

With the exception of the effect of an exogenous shift in the capital supply function, definitive signs are found for the comparative static derivatives of the exogenous variables.[17] The investment model produces results consistent with intuitive judgment and results typically found in other portfolio models. The domestic employment of factors $(I_1$ and $L_1)$ and

Table 2. Comparative Static Analysis—Investment Model

Endogenous Variables	Exogenous Variables								
	P_1	W_1	r	$\overline{eP_2}$	$\overline{eW_2}$	σ^2_{ep}	σ^2_{ew}	σ^2_{epew}	b
L_1	+	−	−[a]	−	+	+	+	−	+
I_1	+	−	−[a]	−	+	+	+	−	+
L_2	−	+	−[a]	+	−	−	−	+	−
I_2	−	+	−[a]	+	−	−	−	+	−

[a] As r' approaches zero.

Note on the use of this table: A positive sign indicates that the *endogenous* variable will change in the *same* direction as the change in the *exogenous* variable. A negative sign indicates that the *endogenous* variable responds in the *opposite* direction to the change in the *exogenous* variable.

consequently the level of production (Q_1) are shown to be positively related to the price of output (P_1), and negatively related to wage costs (W_1). As domestic prices increase, or as domestic wage costs are reduced, domestic profitability is enhanced, and the firm responds by increasing its domestic investment and input levels $(I_1$ and $L_1)$ and the level of domestic output (Q_1). In a similar fashion, foreign factor employment $(I_2$ and $L_2)$ and foreign production (Q_2) are positively related to the expected price of output (eP_2) and negatively related to expected wage costs (eW_2).

The positive slope of the capital supply function serves to relate the consideration of investment opportunities in the two separate markets. As profitability in one market is increased, the desired level of investment is increased. The desired increase in firm-wide investment levels causes the cost of capital to rise. Investment levels in the other "competing" market are then reduced in response to the rise in the firms' cost of capital. As a result, activity levels $(I_i, L_i,$ and $Q_i)$ of each market rise with increases in the profitability of that market, but fall in response to a rise in the profitability of the competing market.

The influence of exogenous change on factor employment totals *firmwide* is indeterminate. As stated above, an increase in marginal profitability in one market increases factor employment and production in that market, while decreasing employment and production in the competing market. As a result, changes in factor employment and production totals for the firm are indeterminate. These results do become determinate under certain conditions.

When the firm's capital supply function is fairly elastic (small increases in the cost of capital associated with large increases in capital investment), the firm is shown to increase total factor employment in response to increases in product prices $(dL/dP_1 > 0, dI/dP_1 > 0, dL/d\overline{eP_2} > 0, dI/d\overline{eP_2} > 0)$. The positive response to increased prices is not offset by the negative influence of a rise in the cost of capital. Firmwide employment and production therefore increases. As the capital supply function becomes increasingly inelastic (the cost of capital rises rapidly as the level of investment increases), the change in total capital and total labor employment becomes ambiguous.

The response of total factor employment to changes in labor costs also becomes determinate when the capital supply function is elastic. Factor employment and production firmwide falls (rises) in response to increases (decreases) in wage costs ($dL/dW_1 < 0$, $dI/dW_1 < 0$, $dL/de\overline{W}_2 < 0$, $dI/de\overline{W}_2 < 0$). The shift of factor employment to the lower cost market does not compensate for the negative influence of the initial increase in labor costs.

An exogenous shift in the capital supply function ($dr^0 \lessgtr 0$) has ambiguous effects. The shift represents a change in the cost of capital at all levels of capital usage. This can be caused by a change in market interest rates, a change in the cost of capital goods, or by a change in technology. The ambiguity results from two possibly conflicting influences. As the cost of capital rises, there is a shift to the usage of labor relative to the usage of capital.[18] At the same time, there is a relative shift of new investment from the lower productivity market to the higher productivity market.[19] The net result is ambiguity regarding the effect of an exogenous shift in the capital supply function on equilibrium input levels.

This ambiguity is resolved as the capital supply function becomes horizontal (r' approaches zero), thereby reducing the incentive to shift new capital between the markets, leaving only a pure "income" effect. As a result, an exogenous increase (decrease) in the cost of capital unambiguously reduces (increases) activity levels (L_1, I_1, L_2, I_2) in both markets.

Activity in both markets is shown to be sensitive to foreign exchange risk. As exchange risk rises, as measured by the variance of foreign prices or of foreign wages, domestic activity rises at the expense of foreign activity. The results of the two-country model have important implications for firm behavior. As exchange risk rises, the risk-averse firm shifts the allocation of capital investment from the foreign market to the risk-insulated domestic market. This is demonstrated by reductions in foreign investment levels in response to increases in the variance of foreign prices, σ^2_{ep}, and the variance of foreign wages, σ^2_{ew} ($dI_2/d\sigma^2_{ep}$ 0, $dI_2/d\sigma^2_{ew} < 0$). Correspondingly, domestic investment is shown to rise in response to increases in the variance of foreign prices, σ^2_{ep}, and the variance of foreign wages, σ^2_{ew}. Labor employment and production, as related to capital investment, is also found to fall (rise) in the foreign (domestic) market in response to a rise in the level of exchange risk.

The related nature of foreign prices and wages is recognized by the covariance term which is negatively entered in the variance-of-profit term. (See equation 4.05.) The variance term is lower to the extent that foreign prices and wages are positively correlated with respect to exchange-rate changes. This correlation (when positive) reduces the negative impact of exchange risk on direct investment and the level of foreign activity.

The response of firmwide factor employment to changing risk conditions is ambiguous. If, however, we assume a near horizontal capital supply function, factor employment totals are shown to decrease in response to increases in exchange risks. Total labor employment and total capital employment fall in response to an increase in the variance of foreign prices and/or to an increase in the variance of foreign wages. An increase in the covariance of eP_2 and eW_2 reduces overall risk and leads to an increase in factor employment totals.

The firm's decisions are also sensitive to the tradeoff between risk and return implicit in the utility function. An increase in the degree of risk aversion, b, shifts activity from the risk-exposed foreign market to the risk-insulated domestic market.[20] Total factor employment (L,I) decreases as the degree of risk aversion rises.

Summary and Conclusions

To summarize briefly, a model of the firm is postulated whereby the firm explicitly determines the level of investment and labor employment in each of two markets. The source of uncertainty in the model consists of the exchange rate and its impact on local-currency prices and wages. The firm's decisions are consistent with the expected utility maximization of a concave quadratic function of profit. Decisions are shown to be sensitive to the expected level and variance of profits.

Comparative static analysis shows that activity levels in a market are positively related to profitability in that market and negatively related to profitability in the "competing" market. Furthermore, the model demonstrates that foreign activity is negatively related to the degree of exchange risk, with the converse true for the domestic market. Total factor employment increases with exogenous changes that increase profitability and decreases with changes that increase risk, assuming a shallow slope for the capital supply function. Finally, all activity levels and the comparative static derivatives are found to be sensitive to the value of b, the degree of risk aversion.

The investment portfolio model presented in this chapter demonstrates several results. Direct foreign investment is shown to be influenced by the profitability of the foreign market, the domestic market, and the level of exchange risk. An interesting result not generally discussed is the sensitivity of domestic investment to risk and profitability in the foreign market. The model is also used to draw conclusions regarding labor employment and exchange risk. These results are apparent, but not typically found in the literature.

The model presented in this chapter differs in several respects from existing models of exchange risk and direct investment. Models typically found in the literature use a capital asset pricing model to derive investment decision rules for the firm. These models are inappropriate for real asset decisions in a world where an international risk-free asset does not exist and when international asset markets are imperfect.

The model presented here uses a measure of exchange risk which is related to the variance of translated foreign prices and wages. Models which utilize the variance of exchange rates as a proxy for exchange risk tend to be misleading in the suggestion that simple hedging operations can eliminate the uncertainty in cash flows. Such specifications are commonplace in the literature.

In addition, the specifications used here acknowledge the interrelationships between exchange-rate-induced price changes and wage changes. When price and wage movements are positively correlated, exchange risk is reduced and the attractiveness of direct investment is enhanced. A negative correlation has the opposite effect. As discussed in the previous chapter, the magnitude and direction of the movement between prices and exchange rates can be estimated from a review of the competition facing the firm in its input and output markets.

The basic model yields intuitively appealing results with a minimum of assumptions and a specification of exchange risk which is broader than that generally found in existing models. The model enables conclusions to be drawn regarding the relationship of domestic and foreign investment, employment, and production to relative profitability, investor preferences, and exchange risk.

5

Currency Denomination of Debt

Introduction

One of the important decisions facing the multinational firm is to determine where to raise funds to finance new capital investment. In a perfectly integrated, certain, and tax-free world, the firm would be indifferent as to where and in what form financial capital is raised.[1] However, in such a world, all forms of capital would be equivalently priced, with respect to the currency in which it is denominated. All market participants would have complete knowledge of the marketplace. The "under-pricing" or "over-pricing" of capital would not occur. In this world of certainty, the currency of denomination is not of significance since exchange rates are fixed, and any future adjustments are known. Decisions such as the currency denomination is not of significance since exchange rates are fixed, and any future adjustments are known. Decisions such as the currency denomination of funds or the form in which to raise capital, are, in fact, mundane and are of no consequence to the firm.

As we begin to introduce reality, these decisions regain their importance. In a less than perfect, taxed, segmented, and uncertain world, several issues arise concerning the firms' financial decisions. These financial issues include the form in which capital should be raised (debt or equity), the term structure of the firms' liabilities, and the currency denomination of the firms' financial instruments. This chapter addresses the factors involved in determining the currency denomination of the firms' financial liabilities.

The discussion in this chapter is limited to decisions involving the financing of capital (physical) investment needs. Capital investment needs are broadly defined to include plant and equipment expenditures, the supply of working capital, and the financing of inventories. It is recognized, however, that the firm may engage in financial transactions for purposes other than meeting its capital needs.

Occasions may arise in the international financial markets where (apparently) profitable arbitrage opportunities exist. These opportunities arise if the financial markets are illiquid or controlled, or if the firm has or believes it has information not reflected in market prices. In response to these opportunities, the firm may speculate, actively engage in covered or uncovered arbitrage, or borrow funds in subsidized capital markets.[2]

Decisions regarding profit opportunities in the financial markets should be evaluated in accordance with operating policies specifically related to such matters. These decisions should be considered independently of real asset decisions and the financing decisions related to the funding of real asset acquisitions. The financing decisions discussed in this chapter are limited to those required to finance real capital investment.

Much of the literature in this area considers financial decisions to be independent of real asset decisions. Stevens (1972) adopts this posture by citing the Modigliani-Miller theorem: with perfect market conditions, financial decisions have no effect on market values, and therefore, they can be made independent of real asset decisions.

Studies which use a capital asset pricing model (Wuster, 1978; Mehra, 1978) are forced to consider these decisions separately. For investment decisions, firms are required to compare the expected return on an asset to the market-implied cost of capital. For financial decisions, the firm is required to compare the expected cost of issuing a financial liability to the market-implied cost of capital. The use of a capital asset pricing rule precludes the firm from recognizing the related nature of risks on its financial and real assets.[3]

Jucker and deFaro (1975) use a portfolio selection model to determine the optimal distribution of international borrowing sources. The model used by Jucker and deFaro is limited to considering financial risks, and also ignores the interrelated nature of risks among different asset types. To quote:

> The source selection problem, as defined here, is a 'pure' financing problem. It does not include consideration of changes, other than changes in borrowing costs, that a firm may face as a result of currency devaluation. Thus, strictly speaking, our model is applicable only by firms that are multinational in but one sense, the potential for sourcing debt funds. Ownership, markets, and factors of production are all assumed to be local to the country of the firm and independent of exchange rate fluctuations (Jucker and deFaro, 1975, p. 382).

The model developed in this chapter permits the financial and real asset decisions to be considered simultaneously. This enables the firm to recognize the interrelated nature of risks between assets. If, for example, the firm finds its local-currency profit flows insensitive to exchange-rate movements (the domestic-currency value fluctuates directly with the exchange rate), it would be desirable from the standpoint of risk to denominate its liabilities in the local currency. This would reduce the amount of local-currency income to be converted to domestic currency, thereby lowering overall corporate risk. If, however, local-currency costs and prices fully adjust to currency fluctuations (a PPP condition), the addition of foreign-currency-denominated liabilities would *introduce* an element of risk to the firms' profit flows.

The risks associated with foreign-currency-denominated liabilities depend on the volatility of exchange rates and the risk-return characteristics of the firms' foreign-currency revenue and cost flows. The risks associated with direct foreign investment also depend on these characteristics as well as on the volatility in costs associated with foreign-currency-denominated liabilities.

In essence, a portfolio model is postulated, with the portfolio composed of foreign and domestic real assets, and foreign and domestic financial liabilities. Portfolios differ in their composition of domestic and foreign assets and liabilities, and this, in turn, affects the risk-return characteristics of the portfolios. The firm selects the portfolio which maximizes utility. In selecting a portfolio, the firm has selected the optimal levels of domestic and foreign capital investment and the optimal currency distribution of the associated liabilities.

A Model of Direct Investment and Foreign-Currency Debt

In the previous chapter, financial capital was assumed to be raised domestically. The financing of investment had a cost consideration only. In the present chapter, risk is introduced to the financing decision by permitting funds to be denominated in the local currency. The funding decision is influenced by the same set of factors which influence the firms' investment decision: risk preferences and the variables which define the risk-return frontier facing the firm.

The firm chooses among portfolios. Each portfolio is represented by levels of domestic and foreign labor employment, domestic and foreign capital employment, and levels of domestic and foreign financial liabilities. When the firm chooses a portfolio, it simultaneously selects the level of all six stocks.

The model presented in this chapter requires the simultaneous determination of five decision variables: investment levels in both markets (I_1, I_2), labor employment in both markets (L_1, L_2), and the proportion of financial capital to be raised in the foreign market (α).

The level of funds available to the firm is assumed to be limited and predetermined. This assumption is consistent with the view of the firm previously expressed. It was argued that in the short run, the firm has limited access to financial capital, due primarily to the risk-averse preferences of lenders and investors. This limited access was previously modeled by assuming a positively sloped capital supply function (in chapter 3) or a positively sloped supply of funds function (in chapter 4).

In this chapter, it is assumed that the firms' present-period financial and economic status, represented by an existing portfolio of assets and liabilities, determines the level of funds available for present-period capital investment. Factors which would be considered by lenders and investors in determining the level of funds include the earning capacity of existing assets, the structure of liabilities, the degree of volatility in net earnings, the ratio of debt to equity, the "track-record" of management, and so forth. Entering the present period, these factors become historical data. Lenders and investors evaluate this historical information and then determine the level of financial capital (D) they are willing to make available for the firms' present period use.

Incorporating an exogenously determined level of financing requires the addition of a constraint condition.[4] This is stated as follows:

$$I = D$$

where $I = I_1 + I_2$

D = level of available funds

The per-unit cost of capital, r, can now be treated as a constant, rather than as a function of the level of capital investment, since the available level of capital is now assumed to be fixed. The costs and risks associated with the level of capital investment are stated in terms of the level of funds, D, to be borrowed by the firm.

In this study, consideration is limited to the currency denomination of *debt obligations*. The risk to the firm arises from the fixed requirement of repayment. The issuance of debt limits the operating freedom of the firm by necessitating a periodic and predetermined cash outflow, regardless of the operating environment present at the time of repayment. The risks to the firm differ with the currency denomination of the debt obligations and the currency characteristics of the firms' other cost and revenue flows.

The payment of dividends to equity holders is made at the discretion of management. The nominal and exchange-rate-adjusted value of dividend payments are not legally guaranteed by the firm. As such, the issuance of equity does not expose the firm to risks similar to those associated with the issuance of debt instruments. Therefore, for purposes of this study, it is assumed that the firm finances all physical investment through the issuance of debt instruments.

Funds raised in the domestic (foreign) market are denominated in the domestic (foreign) currency with all interest payments paid in the domestic (foreign) currency. The term of the debt is assumed to correspond to the useful life of the capital assets acquired. This eliminates consideration of the term structure of the firm's risk exposure.

In equilibrium, it is assumed that the Fisher effect holds, or that interest rates across countries are equal when adjusted for expected exchange-rate changes. This can be stated as follows:

$$r_1 = r_2 + E(\dot{e})$$

where e = currency one price of a unit of currency two

$$\dot{e} = \frac{1}{e}\frac{de}{dt} = \text{rate of change of } e$$

For computational simplicity, it is assumed that $E(\dot{e}) = 0$, or that nominal interest rates are equal in both countries. This does not imply that foreign borrowing is without risk since the exchange rate can still fluctuate $(E(\dot{e}^2) \neq 0)$.

The firm is required to finance its capital investment needs externally. The firm chooses the proportion of those requirements (α) to be denominated in foreign currency. With α selected, both domestic and foreign liability stocks are found, $(1-\alpha)$ D and αD, respectively.[5]

Profits for the firm are given by expression 5.00 below:[6]

$$\tilde{\pi} = P_1Q_1(K_1+I_1,L_1) + \tilde{e}\tilde{P}_2(e)Q_2(K_2+I_2,L_2) - W_1L_1 \qquad 5.00$$

$$- \tilde{e}\tilde{W}_2(e)L_2 - (1-\alpha)rD - \tilde{e}\alpha rD$$

Profits are a composite of revenues from the domestic and foreign markets (P_1Q_1 and eP_2Q_2) respectively, net of domestic and foreign labor costs (W_1L_1 and eW_2L_2) respectively, and net of capital financing costs. The cost of domestically-issued liabilities is given by $(1-\alpha)rD$ with the remainder of the financing burden financed in the foreign market, $e\alpha rD$. Uncertainty is caused by the varying nature of $e,P_2(e)$ and $W_2(e)$. This causes uncertainty in foreign-market revenue flows, foreign labor costs, and the cost of foreign financial liabilities.[7]

The expected value of the profit flow is given in 5.01 below:

$$\overline{\pi} = P_1Q_1(K_1+I_1,L_1) + \overline{eP}_2(e)Q_2(K_2+I_2,L_2) - W_1L_1 \qquad 5.01$$

$$- \overline{eW}_2(e)L_2 - (1-\alpha)rD - \overline{e}\alpha rD$$

The variance of the profit flow, termed economic exchange risk, or economic exposure, is given by 5.02 below:

$$\sigma_\pi^2 = Q_2^2(K_2+I_2,L_2)\sigma_{ep}^2 + L_2^2\sigma_{ew}^2 + \alpha^2r^2D^2\sigma_e^2 \qquad 5.02$$

$$- 2Q_2(K_2+I_2,L_2)L_2\sigma_{epew}^2 - 2Q_2(K_2+I_2,L_2)r\alpha D\sigma_{epe}^2$$

$$+ 2L_2r\alpha D\sigma_{ewe}^2$$

Corporate exposure to risk, as defined by expression 5.02, arises from three sources. The risk from foreign revenues is given by $Q_2^2\sigma_{ep}^2$; and the risk from foreign wage liabilities is given by $L_2^2\sigma_{ew}^2$; and the risk from foreign-currency-denominated financial liabilities is given by $\alpha^2r^2D^2\sigma_e^2$. Changes in the domestic-currency value of these flows are not independently determined, as reflected by the three covariance terms in the corporate-risk expression.

When costs and revenues are positively correlated, overall corporate risk is reduced. The effect on corporate profits is minimized as costs and revenues simultaneously fall or rise in response to exchange-rate changes. Corporate risk falls with a positive correlation between prices and wages ($\sigma_{epew}^2 > 0$) and with a positive correlation between prices and financing costs ($\sigma_{epe}^2 > 0$).

A negative correlation between wage and financing costs also serves to stabilize corporate profits. Total costs and consequently corporate profits remain stable if one cost component rises while another cost component falls in response to exchange-rate adjustments. A negative correlation between wages and financing costs ($\sigma_{ewe}^2 < 0$) reduces corporate risk.

The additional risk associated with foreign-currency-denominated liabilities is identified in 5.03 below:

$$\sigma_\alpha^2 = \alpha^2r^2\sigma_e^2 - 2Q_2(K_2+I_2,L_2)r\alpha D\sigma_{epe}^2 \qquad 5.03$$

$$+ 2L_2r\alpha D\sigma_{ewe}^2$$

In certain circumstances σ_α^2 could be negative. This indicates that the addition of foreign currency debt would reduce overall corporate risk. One plausible example is when local-currency revenues and costs are invariant with respect to exchange-rate changes (σ_{epe}^2 and σ_{ewe}^2 approach σ_e^2). In this situation, the domestic value of these flows fluctuates directly with the rate of exchange. An increase in α would reduce the amount of foreign-currency income to be translated, thereby lowering overall risk.

The additional risk (positive or negative) associated with foreign-currency debt tends to zero as the proportion of foreign liabilities, α, tends to zero. When α is zero, σ_α^2 becomes zero, and σ_π^2 collapses to $Q_2^2\sigma_{ep}^2 + L_2^2\sigma_{ew}^2 - 2Q_2L_2\sigma_{epew}^2$. This is identical to the risk expression in the previous model (4.07).

The problem for the firm is to select the optimal values of L_1, I_1, L_2, I_2 and α which maximize expected utility. The firm must also be aware of the need to invest within the bounds of its capital asset budget. This requires the selected levels of I_2 and I_2 be set equal to D.[8] The maximization problem is now a "constrained" one. Mathematically, this requires the maximization of a Lagrangian function, with the Lagrangian multiplier (λ) being treated as the sixth independent variable.

The objective function must now incorporate a constraint condition to insure that the level of investment used in production (I_1+I_2) equals the amount of funds available to the firm (D).

The problem for the firm is stated as follows:

Maximize $E(U) = \overline{\pi} - b\sigma_\pi^2$

$\quad \overline{\pi}, \sigma_\pi$

Subject to $I = D$

This is transformed into the following Lagrangian expression:

Maximize $\mathcal{L} = P_1Q_1(K_1+I_1, L_1)$

$\quad L_1, I_1, L_2, I_2, \alpha$

$$+ \overline{e}P_2Q_2(K_2+I_2, L_2) - W_1L_1$$

$$- \overline{e}W_2L_2 - \overline{e}r\alpha D - (1-\alpha)rD$$

$$- b[Q_2^2(K_2+I_2, L_2)\sigma_{ep}^2$$

$$+ L_2^2\sigma_{ew}^2 + r^2\alpha^2D^2\sigma_e^2$$

$$- 2Q_2(L_2, K_2+I_2)L_2\sigma_{epew}^2$$

$$- 2Q_2(K_2+I_2, L_2)r\alpha D\sigma_{epe}^2$$

$$+ 2L_2r\alpha D\sigma_{ewe}^2]$$

$$+ \lambda(I-D)$$

The problem now becomes one of selecting the equilibrium level of six variables which maximize the value of 5.03. These variables include the five decision variables plus λ, the Lagrange multiplier.[9]

The first-order conditions are given by 5.04 through 5.09 below:

$$P_1Q_{L_1} - W_1 = 0 \qquad\qquad 5.04$$

$$P_1Q_{I_1} + \lambda = 0 \qquad\qquad 5.05$$

$$\overline{eP_2}Q_{L_2} - \overline{eW_2} - 2bQ_2Q_{L_2}\sigma_{ep}^2 \qquad\qquad 5.06$$
$$- 2bL_2\sigma_{ew}^2 + 2bQ_{L_2}L_2\sigma_{epew}^2$$
$$+ 2bQ_{L_2}r\alpha D\sigma_{epe}^2 - 2br\alpha D\sigma_{ewe}^2 = 0$$

$$\overline{eP_2}Q_{I_2} - 2bQ_2Q_{I_2}\sigma_{ep}^2 + 2bQ_{I_2}L_2\sigma_{epew}^2 \qquad\qquad 5.07$$
$$+ 2bQ_{I_2}r\alpha D\sigma_{epe}^2 + \lambda = 0$$

$$-\overline{er}D + rD - 2br^2\alpha D^2\sigma_e^2 \qquad\qquad 5.08$$
$$+ 2bQ_2rD\sigma_{epe}^2 - 2bL_2rD\sigma_{ewe}^2 = 0$$

$$I - D = 0 \qquad\qquad 5.09$$

Interpretation of First-Order Conditions

Equation 5.04 requires domestic labor to be employed to the point where its marginal revenue product is equal to its marginal cost. Equation 5.06 states that foreign labor be hired to the point where the expected excess of the marginal revenue product over marginal cost is equal to the marginal addition to corporate risk caused by the employment of foreign labor. Conditions 5.05 and 5.07 considered together imply that the marginal revenue product of capital employed in the domestic market be set equal to the expected marginal revenue product of capital in the second market discounted by the marginal increase in corporate risk caused by direct foreign investment.

Dividing 5.08 through by D, we find that the firm should select the proportion of foreign-denominated funds (α) which equates the expected difference in the cost of funds ($r - \overline{er}$) with the marginal increase in corporate risk caused by raising funds in the foreign market ($2br^2\alpha D\sigma_e^2 - 2bQ_2r\sigma_{epe}^2 + 2bL_2r\sigma_{ewe}^2$).

Equation 5.08 clarifies the conditions for the firm to raise funds in the foreign market. If the foreign denomination of liabilities increases risk

$(2br^2\alpha D\sigma_e^2 -2bQ_2r\sigma_{epe}^2 +2bL_2r\sigma_{ewe}^2 > 0)$, the firm would raise foreign funds only if they have a lower expected cost than domestic funds $(\bar{e}r < r)$. The firm would only be willing to pay a higher cost for foreign funds $(\bar{e}r > r)$ in the event that foreign liabilities reduce overall corporate risk $(2br^2\alpha D\sigma_e^2 -2bQ_2r\sigma_{epe}^2 +2bL_2r\sigma_{ewe}^2 < 0)$. Condition 5.09 is a reinstatement of the constraint condition requiring the total level of capital investment (I_1+I_2) to equal the level of financial capital (D) available to the firm.

Comparative Static Results

By exogenously determining the supply of funds available to the firm, the total cost of funds becomes fixed. This effectively reduces the interaction of the model caused by consideration of capital costs. The first-order conditions for I_1 and I_2 reflect this. In making investment decisions, the firm need only compare marginal revenue products and marginal additions to corporate risk for each investment. Previously, these values were also compared to the marginal cost of capital which fluctuated with the level of capital employment. Consideration of the effect of labor employment on the cost of capital is also eliminated since a change in labor employment no longer affects the cost of capital.[10] This would have previously caused a series of second-round adjustments to take place. The increased simplicity of interactions permits more definitive results to be developed.[11]

Inspection of table 3 indicates results that are consistent with those presented in the previous model. The effect of change in prices (P_1) or wages (W_1) in the domestic market have the expected effects on input usage. An increase in domestic profitability, through an increase in prices or a fall in wages, increases domestic input usage (L_1,I_1) while decreasing foreign input usage (L_2,I_2). The firm reacts to increased domestic profitability by shifting its emphasis to the domestic market. Foreign input levels (L_2,I_2) are positively related to exogenous variables which increase the profitability of the foreign market and are negatively related to variables which increase the profitability of the domestic market.

Domestic input variables are positively related to exogenous variables which increase corporate risk, while foreign input variables are negatively related to the same variables. This implies that changes in the operating environment that enhance risk will cause a shift of resources and production from the foreign market to the domestic market.

Total capital employment is invariant with respect to changes in exogenous variables since total investment levels are exogenously determined. Changes in the total labor employment firm-wide (L_1+L_2) with respect to changes in exogenous variables are found to be indeterminate. The only exceptions are an exogenous change in the cost of capital which does not affect labor employment (since the capital stock remains fixed) and an increase (decrease) in the supply of investment funds which unambiguously increases (decreases) total labor employment.

Of particular interest here are the results associated with the decision variable α, and the exogenous parameters σ_{epe}^2, σ_e^2, and σ_{ewe}^2. Inspection of derivatives involving these variables provides information regarding the financing issues raised in the beginning of this chapter.

As table 3 indicates, the decision regarding where to denominate liabilities is influenced by the location of the firms' activities. Changes in parameters which shift activity from the foreign to the domestic market also cause the firm to shift the denomination of its liabilities from the foreign currency to the domestic currency. This is demonstrated by the negative relationship between α and variables which increase domestic profitability ($d\alpha/dP_1 < 0$, $d\alpha/dw_1 > 0$) and the positive relationship of α to variables which enhance foreign profitability ($d\alpha/de\overline{P}_2 > 0$, $d\alpha/de\overline{W}_2 < 0$). These results are consistent with discussions which appear in much of the finance and management literature. Management is generally encouraged to match the location of liabilities to the location of its assets. Part of this advice is political; firms can renege on foreign liabilities if assets are expropriated. But part of this advice is consistent with the firms' attempt to manage its foreign exchange risk exposure. These results are also consistent with the findings reported in Hartman (1979).

The introduction of foreign-currency-denominated liabilities affects the nature of risks associated with direct foreign investment. Foreign-currency-denominated liabilities are fixed in terms of local-currency repayments, but the domestic value of these liabilities fluctuates with changes in exchange rates. The uncertainty in the domestic value of these liabilities may increase or decrease total corporate risk. This relationship depends on the variance of the exchange rate σ_e^2, the covariance of the exchange rate with eP_2, σ_{epe}^2, and the covariance of the exchange rate with eW_2, σ_{ewe}^2.[12]

An increase in the variance of the exchange rate increases the risk associated with the repayment of foreign liabilities. The response is to shift resource usage from the foreign to the domestic market, including the proportion of the liabilities to be denominated in the domestic currency ($dL_1/d\sigma_e^2 > 0$, $dI_1/d\sigma_e^2 > 0$, $dL_2/d\sigma_e^2 < 0$, $dI_2/d\sigma_e^2 < 0$, $d\alpha/d\sigma_e^2 < 0$). The variance of the exchange rate, frequently but inappropriately termed exchange risk, is shown to influence foreign operations. Increases in exchange rate volatility increases the risk associated with foreign financing, thereby directing the firm to reduce the equilibrium levels of foreign investment, employment, and liabilities.

As discussed previously, increases in the covariance between foreign financing costs and foreign revenues (σ_{epe}^2) reduce overall risk. This occurs because rising (falling) revenues offset rising (falling) costs, keeping margins relatively stable. This model is able to demonstrate the effect of this risk reduction, showing conclusively that foreign activity increases while domestic activity levels are reduced as the covariance term increases ($dL_1/d\sigma^2_{epe} < 0$, $dI_1/d\sigma^2_{epe} < 0$, $dL_2/d\sigma^2_{epe} > 0$, $dI_2/d\sigma^2_{epe} > 0$, $d\alpha/d\sigma^2_{epe} > 0$).

The covariant movement of foreign financing costs with foreign wage costs increases overall risk as both costs rise (fall) with respect to increases (decreases) in the exchange rate. Accordingly, a decrease in the covariance term σ^2_{ewe} reduces corporate risk and is negatively related to L_1 and I_1, and positively related to L_2, I_2, and α.

Exogenous changes in the cost of capital, r, have no effect on the equilibrium levels of the input variables. This is because maximization takes place with the level of financial capital predetermined. In essence, changes in r are treated as a change in a fixed cost, therefore not affecting the equilibrium levels of production. Changes in r do, however, affect the risk associated with foreign liabilities. An increase in r reduces profits while increasing the proportion of total costs at risk. In response, the firm should reduce the equilibrium level of foreign denominated liabilities, as indicated by the negative sign of $d\alpha/dr$.

Summary and Conclusions

The issuance of foreign-currency-denominated financial liabilities involves risk. This risk is not independent of the exchange risk associated with foreign real assets or foreign labor employment. Accordingly, decisions regarding direct foreign investment, foreign employment, and foreign-currency-denominated liabilities should be made simultaneously. This permits the firm to gain from its knowledge of the interrelated return structure of these assets and liabilities.

A model has been presented which uses the structure of the previous model, while incorporating consideration of foreign and domestic financing costs. The results of the model are summarized in table 3.

The first-order conditions (equations 5.04 through 5.09) provide the *requirements* necessary for foreign borrowings: borrow in the foreign market if the cost of capital is lower than in the domestic market, or if foreign denominated liabilities *lower* the overall corporate exposure to exchange risk. Comparative-static derivatives indicate that funds should be raised in markets where the firms' activities take place (subject to the above requirements). Changes in the operating environment that cause the firm to shift activity from one market to another also cause the firm to shift the denomination of its liabilities in the same direction.

Risks associated with the currency denomination of debt are also

Table 3. Comparative Static Analysis—Foreign Debt Model

Endogenous Variables	Exogenous Variables											
	P_1	W_1	$\overline{eP_2}$	$\overline{eW_2}$	r	σ_e^2	σ_{ep}^2	σ_{ew}^2	σ_{epew}^2	σ_{epe}^2	σ_{ewe}^2	D
L_1	+	–	–	+	0	+	+	+	–	–	+	+
I_1	+	–	–	+	0	+	+	+	–	–	+	+
L_2	–	+	+	-	0	–	–	–	+	+	–	+
I_2	–	+	+	–	0	–	–	–	+	+	–	+
α	–	+	+	–	–[a]	–	–	–	+	+	–	–

[a] Assumes $\alpha > 0$.

related to the other risks incurred by the firm in its foreign operations. The risk aspects of foreign liabilities are directly related to the variance of the exchange rate. An increase in the volatility of the exchange rate is shown to reduce foreign activity and financing levels, to the benefit of domestic activity and domestic financing levels.

An increasing correlation of foreign financing costs with foreign-source revenues reduces overall corporate risk. A negative correlation between foreign financing costs and foreign labor costs also reduces corporate risk levels. As the degree of these correlations increase, foreign activity variables are increased while domestic activity is shown to decrease.

The results of the foreign debt model are consistent with the findings of the previous model presented. The results provided by this model are also consistent with general discussions found in the existing literature.

6

Exchange Risk and International Trade

Introduction

Previous chapters have focused on issues associated with direct investment. The models used in exploring these issues have assumed that the foreign market could only be supplied from locally-based production with the domestic market supplied from domestic production. In the absence of trade, direct investment became the only vehicle through which the firm could service profitable foreign markets.

How would the results of previous chapters be affected if the assumption of autarky (no trade) is relaxed? The model presented in this chapter permits trade flows between markets. As this chapter demonstrates, the added degree of flexibility permitted by trade flows alters the responses of the firm to external change. In addition, relaxing the assumption of autarky permits an investigation of the effects of tariff policies on the firms' production, investment and trade decisions.

In this chapter, the firm is able to separate its production and sales decisions in each market. Excess production in one market can be exported for sale to the other market, and vice-versa. This formulation more closely resembles the environment facing multinational firms, and permits the exploration of issues involving international trade and exchange risk. As treated throughout this study, the issues raised here are developed from the microeconomic perspective of the multinational firm.

A Model of Exchange Risk and International Trade

In this trade model, the firm selects the utility maximizing level of six stocks: domestic and foreign labor employment (L_1, L_2), domestic and foreign capital investment (I_1, I_2) and domestic and foreign sales (S_1, S_2). The optimal input levels, L_1^*, L_2^*, I_1^*, and I_2^* determine the optimal level of firm-wide production, $Q_1^* + Q_2^*$. Total output is then allocated among the domestic and foreign markets. It is assumed that net inventory accumulation is zero, such that total sales equal total production. This requires the use of a constraint to insure the equality of firm-wide production with firm-wide sales.[1]

Separating the sales and production decisions gives the firm greater flexibility in its operations. As the firm attempts to achieve its objectives, it enjoys a greater range of options for producing in the relatively lower cost/lower risk market while selling in the higher revenue/lower risk market.

In the present model, funds are assumed to be raised domestically. This assumption, as used in chapter 4, serves to simplify the analysis, providing a clearer view of the issues involving trade and exchange risk. As also assumed in chapter 4, capital is employed at increasing cost such that $r'(I) > 0$ with $r''(I) = 0$.

The model used here is a single-period model, as are the prior models presented in this study. The use of a single-period model is sufficient to address the basic issues being raised; in this case, how would the equilibrium levels of the input, output, and sales stocks be altered given any change in the exogenous operating environment. The single-period time frame is considered to be long enough for the firm to plan its investment decisions, but short enough such that exchange risk is a factor for consideration. The view that purchasing power parity is restored in the long run does not prevent exchange risk from being a consideration in the short-term and intermediate-term time frame.

Profits for the firm are given by expression 6.01 below:

$$\tilde{\pi} = P_1 S_1 + \tilde{e}\tilde{P}_2(e)S_2 - W_1 L_1 - \tilde{e}\tilde{W}_2(e)L_2 \qquad\qquad 6.01$$
$$\quad - r(I)I - t[S_2 - Q_2(K_2 + I_2, L_2)]$$

Revenues in 6.01 are given by the sum of $P_1 S_1$ and $\tilde{e}\tilde{P}_2(e)S_2$. The domestic value of foreign sales is uncertain due to the stochastic nature of e and $P_2(e)$. Costs are given by the domestic and foreign wage bills, $W_1 L_1$ and $\tilde{e}\tilde{W}_2(e)L_2$, and the user cost of capital, $r(I)I$. The domestic value of the foreign wage bill is uncertain due to the stochastic nature of e and $W_2(e)$.

An additional term in the profit function, $t[S_2 - Q_2(K_2 + I_2, L_2)]$, allows for tariff issues to be explored. When foreign sales exceed foreign production $(S_2 > Q_2)$, the deficit is supplied from domestic production. The imposition of an import tariff reduces corporate profits by the tariff (t) multiplied by the number of units imported, $S_2 - Q_2$.[2] When foreign production exceeds foreign sales, the firm exports its surplus production to the domestic market and t is set to zero.

The tariff term t can be viewed, generally, as a tax on the flow of resources across borders. The tariff could be levied as an actual tax on goods, or could be extracted in more subtle ways. For example, the tariff term could represent a cost penalty created by currency controls or in a similar manner, as a cost penalty created by import quotas.

Effective currency controls limit the ability of the firm to obtain foreign currency as needed for the payment of imported resources. In many cases the firm pays a surcharge to the government to obtain foreign currency by purchasing the currency at a differential (import) rate of exchange. The firm could also acquire the currency on the open market, but at a rate above the "official" rate of exchange.

In these instances, effective currency controls create a cost penalty when foreign currency or foreign goods are to be acquired. There are many ways to model this financially. For our purposes, the situation can be construed as trade occurring at market prices and transacted at the official rate of exchange, but with a tariff being levied on the importation of goods.

With a little ingenuity, import quotas can be modelled in a similar fashion. When import quotas are non-binding (the firm wishes to import less than its allowed quota), the quotas are of little concern.[3] If the quotas are effective by limiting the firm from carrying out its desired plans, then certain financial considerations arise. In our model, a quota can be viewed as a tariff on the importation of goods. To make this assumption, the firm should be able to purchase from the government or on the market, additional quota allocations. The cost of the quota allocations can be treated as an import tariff.[4] The exposure of the profit flow to exchange risk is given by the variance term in 6.02 below:

$$\sigma_\pi^2 = S_2^2\sigma_{ep}^2 + L_2^2\sigma_{ew}^2 - 2L_2S_2\sigma_{epew}^2 \qquad\qquad 6.02$$

The risk term in 6.02 differs from that of previous models as the level of risk is sensitive to the level of sales and the level of production. In previous models, sales and production levels were equivalent. Viewing the extremes, if all foreign sales were supplied by imports, L_2 would be zero and corporate risk would equal $S_2^2\sigma_{ep}^2$, the risk associated with the domestic value of foreign revenues. At the other extreme, if all foreign production is exported, S_2 would be zero and corporate risk is limited to $L_2^2\sigma_{ew}^2$, the risk associated with the uncertainty of the foreign wage bill.

The problem for the firm is to select the utility maximizing levels of L_1, I_1, L_2, I_2, S_1, and S_2. Total sales must equal total production firm-wide, requiring the following constraint condition be satisfied:

$$S_1 + S_2 = Q_1(K_1 + I_1, L_1) + Q_2(K_2 + I_2, L_2)$$

The utility function assumed is the same employed in previous chapters:

$$\text{Maximize } U = \overline{\pi} - b\sigma_\pi^2$$
$$\overline{\pi}, \sigma_\pi$$

This is transformed into the Lagrangian expression given by 6.03 below:

$$\text{Maximize } \mathcal{L} = P_1 S_1 + e\overline{P}_2(e)S_2 - W_1 L_1 \qquad\qquad 6.03$$
$$L_1, I_1, L_2, I_2,$$
$$S_1, S_2, \lambda$$

$$- t[S_2 - Q_2(K_2 + I_2, L_2)]$$
$$- b[S_2^2 \sigma_{ep}^2 + L_2^2 \sigma_{ew}^2 - 2L_2 S_2 \sigma_{epew}^2]$$
$$- \lambda[S_1 + S_2 - Q_1(K_1 + I_1, L_1) - Q_2(K_2 + I_2, L_2)]$$

The following are the (first-order) conditions which need to be satisfied to arrive at the optimal values of the variables in question.[5]

$$\lambda Q_{L_1} - W_1 = 0 \qquad\qquad 6.04$$

$$\lambda Q_{I_1} - r'I - r = 0 \qquad\qquad 6.05$$

$$\lambda Q_{L_2} + t Q_{L_2} - e\overline{W}_2 - 2bL_2\sigma_{ew}^2 \qquad\qquad 6.06$$
$$+ 2bS_2\sigma_{epew}^2 = 0$$

$$\lambda Q_{I_2} + t Q_{I_2} - r'I - r = 0 \qquad\qquad 6.07$$

$$P_1 - \lambda = 0 \qquad\qquad 6.08$$

$$e\overline{P}_2 - t - 2bS_2\sigma_{ep}^2 + 2bL_2\sigma_{epew}^2 - \lambda = 0 \qquad\qquad 6.09$$

$$Q_1 + Q_2 - S_1 - S_2 = 0 \qquad\qquad 6.10$$

Interpretation of First-Order Conditions

Consideration of conditions 6.08 and 6.09 together implies that sales levels should be set such that marginal revenue in the domestic market (P_1) equals marginal revenue ($e\overline{P}_2 - t$) in the foreign market discounted for the marginal increase in corporate risk ($2bL_2\sigma_{epew}^2 - 2bS_2\sigma_{ep}^2$). Marginal revenue in the foreign market is equal to the expected selling price net of the tariff (when $t > 0$). These conditions demonstrate that foreign sales are discouraged as the tariff rate is increased in equilibrium. When 6.08 and 6.09 are satisfied, λ represents the marginal utility of a unit increase in sales, irrespective of the market where the additional output is sold. Condition 6.10 is a restatement of the constraint condition requiring total output to equal total sales.

Condition 6.04 requires domestic labor to be employed to the point where the value of the marginal product of labor (λQ_{L_1}) equals its marginal cost (W_1). Condition 6.05 states a similar requirement for the employment of domestic capital. Domestic capital investment should take place up to the point where the value of the marginal product of domestic capital (λQ_{I_1}) is equal to its marginal cost ($r + r'I$).

Condition 6.06 requires foreign labor to be employed to the point where the value of the marginal product of foreign labor ($\lambda Q_{L_2} + t Q_{L_2}$) equals the expected value of the marginal cost of labor ($\overline{eW}_2$) plus the marginal increase in corporate risk due to an increase in L_2, ($2bL_2\sigma_{ew}^2 - 2bS_2\sigma_{epew}^2$). The tariff plays a role in the satisfaction of condition 6.06. When $t>0$, the term $t Q_{L_2}$ is added to condition 6.06 which can be used to balance the marginal costs and marginal increases in risk which are subtracted from 6.06.

A lump-sum tariff (t) is applied to all imports to the foreign market. Imports are given by the difference between foreign sales and foreign production ($S_2 - Q_2$). Therefore, a unit increase in foreign output reduces the firms' tariff liability, or can be viewed as increasing revenues by t. As a result, the imposition of a tariff increases the incentives to increase foreign production and consequently to increase foreign labor employment.

Condition 6.07 holds interesting implications for direct investment. This condition requires the value of the marginal product of foreign investment ($\lambda Q_{I_2} + t Q_{I_2}$) to be set equal to the marginal cost of capital to the firm ($r + r'I$). Condition 6.07, unlike the condition for the employment of foreign labor, contains no risk term associated with the foreign employment of capital.

In essence, 6.07 states that the firm should consider direct investment to be free of exchange risk. There are two reasons for this unusual result. First, the cost of direct investment is known, because of the assumption that all physical capital is financed domestically. This eliminates exchange-risk considerations from the cost of financing the foreign capital investment. Secondly, foreign production is not restricted to be sold in the foreign market. Rather, it becomes the choice of the firm as to where foreign output is sold. Therefore, the firm is able to apportion the risks of foreign sales ($S_2^2\sigma_{ep}^2 - 2S_2L_2\sigma_{epew}^2$) to its sales decision, thereby allowing the firm to consider the foreign employment of capital as being free of exchange risk on the revenue side. Consequently, with riskless financing and the ability to sell in any market, the firm considers direct foreign investment to be free of exchange risks.

This conclusion should be tempered somewhat. Three difficult conditions are required for the foreign operations to be free of exchange risk. First, financing should be denominated in the domestic currency. Second, all inputs required for foreign-located production should have alternative sources in the domestic economy. This becomes quite difficult in the case of labor. Finally, the domestic market should be able to absorb all of the foreign-produced output. If these three requirements are met, the firm has effectively isolated itself from exchange risks since it always has the opportunity to incur all of its foreign operation costs and revenues in domestic currency.

Is there a purpose to direct foreign investment under this stringent set of circumstances? Yes, to the extent that actual operations utilize locally sourced inputs and/or sell products into the local market. To be free of exchange risk requires the ability to operate in the foreign market with domestic inputs and to sell back to the domestic market. It does not require the actuality of a totally "domestic" foreign-located operation.

Comparative Static Results

The separation of the sales and production decisions permits the firm greater flexibility in making its utility maximizing decisions. The firm can more accurately assign risk and return attributes to the endogenous variables, thereby allowing more "efficient" decisions to be made by the firm.

The results of the trade model are keenly sensitive to assumptions regarding $eP_2(e)$ and $eW_2(e)$, the domestic-currency values of foreign prices and foreign wages. The direction and magnitude of changes in these domestic-currency values in response to unanticipated exchange-rate adjustments depends on several factors, as discussed in detail in chapter 3. Of paramount influence is the source and degree of local or world competition in the markets where $P_2(e)$ and $W_2(e)$ are determined.

A similarity of demand conditions in the input and output markets results in $eP_2(e)$ and $eW_2(e)$ moving in the same direction in response to unanticipated exchange-rate adjustments. A positive correlation between $eP_2(e)$ and $eW_2(e)$ ($\sigma^2_{epew} > 0$) indicates that profit margins in the foreign market will remain relatively stable when subjected to volatile exchange-rate movements. (See figure 6). This implies that the firm's exposure to exchange risk is limited when σ^2_{epew} is positive.

When demand conditions differ significantly in the input and product markets, the firm finds its profit margins extremely sensitive to unanticipaged exchange-rate changes. A situation typifying this problem arises when output prices are set internationally, but inputs are sourced locally and are insensitive to exchange-rate movements. The firm finds that the domestic

Figure 6. Positive correlations of $eP_2(e)$ and $eW_2(e)$ $(\sigma^2_{epew} > 0)$

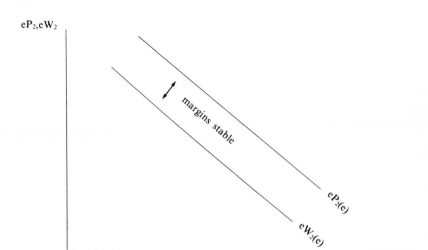

World competition in sales and inputs, margins stable

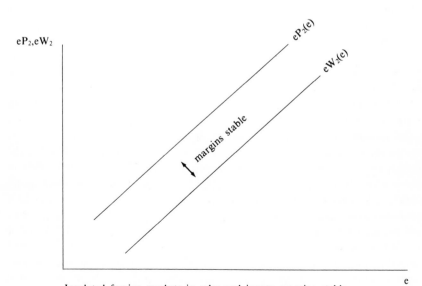

Insulated foreign markets in sales and inputs, margins stable

value of the foreign wage bill increases proportionately with an appreciation of the foreign currency (de$>$0), but the domestic value of the foreign production remains stable or falls slightly as the deflationary impact of a currency appreciation exerts downward pressure on P_2.

At the extreme, differing demand conditions result in eP_2(e) and eW_2(e) moving in different directions in response to changes in e. A negative correlation between these values, as represented by a negative value of σ^2_{epew}, indicates that the foreign-market profit margins are extremely sensitive to exchange-rate movements. (See figure 7.) The firm finds that its exposure to exchange risk rises as σ^2_{epew} becomes increasingly negative.

The results reported in table 4 are based on a set of assumptions which are characteristic of a high degree of "sensitivity" to exchange risk. These conditions assume large values for σ^2_{ep} and σ^2_{ew}, and a negative correlation between eP_2 and eW_2 ($\sigma^2_{epew} < 0$). In many instances, the results require an elastic capital supply function. An asterisk (*) is used to denote those results which would be ambiguous under conditions where the capital supply function is steeply sloped and/or when σ^2_{ep} and σ^2_{ew} are low in value.

The implications of the trade model can also be demonstrated when changes in total sales (S_1+S_2) and changes in net exports (S_2-Q_2) are studied. While this type of analysis tends to simplify the underlying interactions, it does serve to clarify the implications for the firm of exogenous change in the operating environment. Table 5 summarizes the direction of change in total sales and in the level of trade between the domestic and foreign markets. The results reported in table 5 are also conditional on the set of assumptions discussed above.

In permitting trade, the firm's responses to exogenous changes differs significantly from its reactions under conditions of autarky. In the previous models, the firm would shift resources and sales to the market where product prices increased or costs of production fell. Similarly, the firm would shift resources and sales to the foreign market as risk variables declined, or away from the foreign market as measures of exchange risk rose.

In the present model, the firm is able to respond in a more direct fashion to changes in the operating environment. In general, the firm responds to changes in revenue conditions (P_1, $\overline{eP_2}$, σ^2_{ep}) by shifting sales to the more attractive market (higher revenue or lower risk). As the shift in sales alters the firm's exposure to exchange risk, the firm responds by shifting production to the market, thereby "counterbalancing" the change in risk caused by the shift in sales.

In response to higher foreign product prices, the firm shifts sales from the domestic market to the foreign market. The shift in sales to the foreign market increases profitability, but also increases the firm's exposure to exchange risk, assuming a negative correlation between prices and wages. In

Figure 7. Negative correlations of $eP_2(e)$ and $eW_2(e)$ ($\sigma^2_{epew} < 0$)

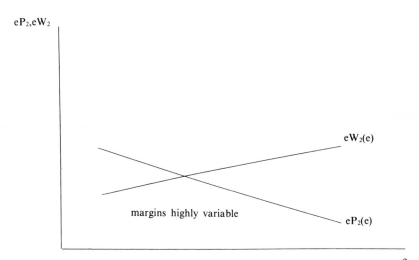

Competition in sales with inputs insulated, margins volatile

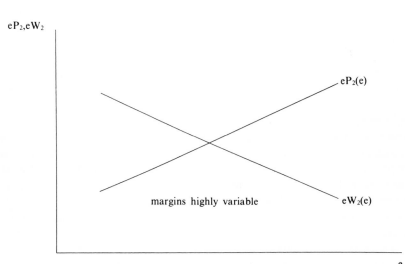

Competition in inputs with sales insulated, margins volatile

Table 4. Comparative Static Analysis—Trade Model

Endogenous Variables	Exogenous Variables									
	P_1	W_1	$\overline{eP}_2$	$\overline{eW}_2$	σ^2_{ep}	σ^2_{ew}	σ^2_{epew}	r^o	t	b
L_1	+*	−	+	+	−	+	−*	−*	−	+1
I_1	+*	−	+	+	−	+	−*	−*	−	+1
L_2	+*	+	−	−	+	−	+*	−*	+	−1
I_2	+*	+	−	−	+	−	+*	−*	+	−1
S_1	+	−*	−*	−*	+*	−*	?	−*	+*	?
S_2	−*	−	+	+	−	+	?	−*	−	?

*Ambiguous for low values of σ^2_{ew} or σ^2_{ep} and/or high value of dr/dl.
1. If σ^2_{ep} and σ^2_{ew} are less than perfectly correlated.

response to the increased exposure, the firm shifts production from the foreign market to the risk-insulated domestic market. The simultaneous responses of higher foreign sales and lower foreign production could not occur without the ability to trade. Again, it is useful to be reminded of the motivating factors, a set of conditions which exposes the firm to significant exchange risks when producing or selling in the local market, and a corporate aversion to risk.

The firms' response to an increase in domestic product prices differs from its response to changes in foreign product prices, but follows a similar logic. The increase in domestic prices causes a shift in sales from the foreign to domestic market. The firm also responds by increasing domestic and foreign production as demonstrated by positive derivatives for all inputs with respect to domestic prices. (See table 5.) The increase in domestic production is required, in part, to meet the higher level of domestic sales. The reduction in foreign sales reduces the firm's exposure to exchange risk, thereby permitting the firm to increase its more profitable but higher-risk foreign production.[6]

An increase in the risk of foreign sales causes the firm to shift sales from the foreign market to the lower-risk domestic market. The shift of sales to the domestic market lowers revenues.[7] The firm responds, in part, by shifting production to the higher margin but higher-risk foreign market. This is evident from the positive response of foreign input usage to increases in σ^2_{ep} and the negative signs for domestic input usage.

The firm's responses can also be viewed in a somewhat different manner. The firm reacts to an increase in σ^2_{ep} by shifting sales to the domestic market. The firm reduces its exposure to risk but also reduces revenues. On the revenue side, the firm lowers both risk and return. On the production side, the firm partially restores profitability by shifting production to the higher-margin market of production, the foreign market.[8] This increases

Table 5. Changes in the Volume of Firm-Wide Sales and Net Exports to the Foreign Market

Endogenous Variables	Exogenous Variables									
	P_1	W_1	$\overline{eP}_2$	$\overline{eW}_2$	σ^2_{ep}	σ^2_{ew}	t^o	σ^2_{epew}	r^o	b
$S^{(1)}$	+	−	−	−	−	−	+	?	−	?
$X_n^{(2)}$	−	−	+	+	−	+	−	?	?	?

Note: These results are based on the assumptions discussed on page 60. Low values of σ^2_{ep}, σ^2_{ew} and/or a steeply sloped capital supply curve would produce ambiguous results.
1. The change in firm-wide sales (dS) is equal to the sum of changes in domestic sales levels, dS_1, and changes in foreign sales levels, dS_2.
2. The change in net-exports (dX_n) is equal to the change in foreign sales, dS_2, minus the change in foreign production, dQ_2. A negative sign for X_n indicates that exports to the foreign market are reduced, or that imports to the domestic market are increased.

exchange risks in the production of output. In essence, the lower risk-return profile in sales is balanced by a higher risk-return profile in production.

The firm's responses to changing production attributes can be explained in a similar light. In response to an exogenous change, the firm balances marginal changes in the risk-return attributes in its production choices, in its sales decisions, and in an overall revenue-production manner. Production attributes include the domestic cost of production, the foreign cost of production, and the risks associated with the foreign wage bill.

An increase in domestic labor costs reduces domestic and foreign sales levels. Lower production requirements reduce domestic production. The lower profitability caused by the increase in domestic production costs, and the lower risks caused by lower foreign sales levels, permits the firm to increase foreign production levels. Higher foreign production partially restores the relationship between corporate risk and profitability, as the higher-margin and higher-risk foreign production in part offsets the reduction in risk and return caused by rising domestic wages.

An increase in the cost of, or risk associated with, the employment of foreign labor has similar effects on the equilibrium levels of the six endogenous stock variables. An increase in $\overline{eW}_2$ or σ^2_{ew} shifts production from the foreign market to the domestic market. In both instances, the risks and returns from production are reduced by the shift. This lower risk-return profile in production permits the firm to increase risks and returns in its sales efforts. Thus, in response to a rise in $\overline{eW}_2$ or σ^2_{ew}, the firm also acts to shift sales from the domestic market to the foreign market.

As discussed previously, an increase in the covariance between foreign prices and wages ($d\sigma^2_{epew} > 0$) tends to reduce corporate risk. As risks are reduced, the firm shifts production from the domestic market to the lower-cost foreign market. A change in the covariance term has an indeterminate effect on equilibrium sales levels in both markets. This indeterminacy can best be explained by the divergent response to cost-associated and revenue-associated risks. The firm increases domestic sales and decreases foreign sales in response to an *increase* in σ_{ep}^2, and in response to a *decrease* in σ_{ew}^2. Consequently, the response of sales levels to an increase in the correlation between σ_{ep}^2 and σ_{ew}^2 is ambiguous.

This ambiguity is also found in the response of equilibrium sales levels to a change in the risk-preference parameter, b. An increase in the degree of risk aversion (db $>$ 0) shifts production from the foreign market to the domestic market. The effect of altering b on equilibrium sales levels is ambiguous. This is consistent with previous conflicting responses of domestic and foreign sales levels with respect to changes in risk parameters.

An exogenous shift in the capital supply function affects all six decision variables in the same direction. A downward shift in the function (dr$^\circ$ $<$ 0) increases capital investment, labor employment, and sales levels in both markets. Correspondingly, all activity and sales variables decrease in response to an exogenous increase in the cost of capital (dr$^\circ$ $>$ 0).

The introduction of trade to the model permits an investigation of the effects of tariff policies on the optimization decisions of the firm. The model as described in 6.00 through 6.03 taxes net imports to the foreign market. The tax is in the form of a lump-sum charge per unit imported. As discussed previously, in certain circumstances this tax can also be considered as a proxy for currency controls or import quotas.

The tariff alters the firm's sales and production incentives, affecting all of the firms' optimization choices. When the firm imports production from the domestic market, each additional unit of foreign sales increases the tariff burden by t. Similarly, each additional unit of foreign production reduces the firm's tariff burden by t. Given this structure of incentives, the firm shifts production to the import market as the tariff burden is increased. This is demonstrated by increases in foreign labor usage and direct investment levels, and by reductions in domestic input usage. The firm also responds by reducing sales in the foreign market, while increasing sales in the domestic market. The dual effect of increasing foreign production while decreasing foreign sales serves to reduce the import gap rapidly. This result is consistent with traditional trade theory which states that the volume of trade decreases as tariff rates rise.[9]

In situations where foreign output increases (dL_2 $>$ 0, dI_2 $>$ 0) and foreign sales fall (dS_2 $<$ 0), exports to the foreign market are reduced, or conceivably imports to the domestic market are increased. In situations where foreign sales increase (dS_2 $>$ 0), while foreign production falls (dL_2 $<$ 0, dI_2 $<$ 0), exports to the foreign market are increased, or domestic imports are decreased. These results are summarized in table 5.

Total sales levels increase when profitability is increased without a corresponding increase in risk levels (an increase in P_1 or reductions in W_1 or r^o). Similarly, total sales are reduced when risk is increased without a corresponding increase in returns (an increase in σ_{ep}^2 or σ_{ew}^2). Total sales are reduced when foreign wages increase, since the rise in foreign wages reduces profitability while at the same time increasing risk.

The effects of changes in foreign prices and tariff rates on total sales levels requires some explanation. An increase in $\overline{eP_2}$ increases both profitability and risk. The increase in profitability is realized by the increase in foreign revenues and sales. The associated increase in risk is ameliorated, in part, by shifting production to the risk-free domestic market. Overall, however, the firm scales back total sales because of its risk-averse preferences. This is shown by the negative sign for $dS/de\overline{P_2}$. In essence, the firm chooses not to enjoy the full increase in profitability made available by the increase in foreign prices. Part of the increase in profits is "rescinded" through the firm's efforts to reduce the increased risk exposure which accompanies the higher foreign prices.

As discussed previously, net exports to the foreign market are reduced as tariff rates rise. This occurs as the tariff alters the effective prices and costs facing the firm. As the tariff rises, net revenues from foreign sales are reduced, and the firm shifts sales to the domestic market. The increased tariff also effectively reduces the cost of producing in the foreign market, since each unit of local production reduces the tariff bill for a given level of local sales. Accordingly, the firm responds by shifting production to the foreign market. The overall effect of a tariff increase on firm-wide sales is to *increase* total sales ($dS/dt^o > 0$).

When changes in the volume of net exports are considered, the responses of the firm to exogenous change are clearly demonstrated. In essence, the firm increases its exports to a market when it becomes more attractive to sell in, or less attractive to produce in, that particular market. As prices rise in the domestic market, net exports from that market are reduced. Rising foreign product prices encourage increased exports to the foreign market. As discussed, an increase in tariff rates discourages domestic exports to the foreign market.

Rising labor costs have the same effect as rising product prices; they encourage exports to the rising-cost market. An increase in W_1 discourages exports to the foreign market, whereas an increase in $\overline{eW_2}$ encourages foreign imports. An increase in the cost of capital reduces all production and sales levels, resulting in an indeterminate effect on net exports.

An inspection of the effects of risk variables on trade patterns also provides interesting conclusions. Statements can be made regarding changes in net exports, but no conclusive statements can be made regarding exchange risk and the absolute volume of trade. An increase in sales-related risks ($d\sigma_{ep}^2$

> 0) reduces the volume of net exports to the foreign market. If the foreign country is a net importer, then an increase in σ_{ep}^2 will reduce imports, and consequently the volume of trade. If the foreign country is a net exporter, exports and the volume of trade will increase with an increase in σ_{ep}^2.

The firm increases net exports to the foreign market as production risks rise ($d\sigma_{ew}^2 > 0$). If the foreign country is in a net-import position, rising production risks increase domestic exports and the volume of trade. If the foreign country is in a net-export position, rising production risks reduce the net-export position and the overall volume of trade.

Summary and Conclusions

This chapter has presented a model which permits the flow of goods between markets. The introduction of trade allows the firm to separate its production and sales decisions. The model also permits an investigation of tariffs and the effect of exchange risk on international trade.

The model presented in this chapter produces results consistent with traditional trade theory. The introduction of exchange risk considerations does not affect the direction of responses to changing import-tariff rates. As tariffs increase, the firm shifts production to the protected foreign market, but also shifts sales away from the foreign market. Imports are reduced as foreign production rises while foreign sales fall. As the tariff rate rises, marginal revenues fall on foreign sales. Overall, the total volume of trade has been shown to decline as the tariff rate is increased.

In summary, the ability to move production between markets gives the firm greater flexibility in the optimization process. When exposure to exchange risk is an important consideration, the firm is shown to balance risks and returns in sales and production.[10] This balancing effort is most clearly displayed when the effects of exogenous changes on net exports are studied. In previous models the firm could not separate its production and sales decisions. This left the firm with less flexibility to adjust to changing economic conditions.

With trade permitted, the firm is shown to counterbalance risk and return attributes in its sales and production decisions. Factors which lead the firm to reduce risks in production also result in greater exposure to risk in sales, and vice-versa. Conditions which reduce expected returns in sales lead the firm to increase expected returns in production, and vice-versa. On a trade basis, the firm is shown to increase net exports to the market where selling conditions improve or where production conditions deteriorate.

7

Summary and Conclusions

This research effort was motivated, in part, by the volatile nature of the international financial markets over the past decade, in conjunction with a perceived inadequate theoretical treatment of foreign-exchange risk.

In this study, exchange risk has been broadly defined as the uncertainty in the firms' cash flow and market value induced by unanticipated exchange-rate changes. Generally, three broad perspectives have developed regarding the effects of exchange risk on the multinational firm. One view is short-term in nature, considering the risks to be limited to changes in the value of exposed foreign-currency-denominated assets and liabilities, and to changes in the value of outstanding foreign-currency-denominated transactions. At a cost, these forms of exposure can be covered. The second view argues that the firm is not exposed to any risks from changing rates of exchange, since in the long run some form of purchasing power parity will be maintained. A third view, which is shared by the author, argues that deviations from purchasing power parity can exist for significant periods of time, thereby leaving the firm exposed to exchange risk.

The premise underlying this study is that unanticipated exchange-rate changes may alter the supply and demand characteristics of the firms' factor and product markets. The characteristics of these markets may be altered for significant periods of time when deviations from purchasing power parity persist due to imperfect or insulated markets, or as a result of macro-economic policies which produce chronic balance of payments disequilibrium, or when exchange-rate adjustments alter real incomes. The sensitivity of market conditions to exchange-rate changes exposes the firms' cash flow and market value to variation.

Economic exposure to exchange risk arises from the uncertain influence changing exchange rates may have on the revenue and cost structure of the firm. The cost of foreign production may change in response to exchange-rate changes because inputs are imported or, if locally acquired, face inter-national competition. Revenues may change as a result of changing rates of exchange because output is destined for the export market or, if sold locally, may face import competition. Local production fully insulated from the world marketplace may still be exposed because of the income effect of exchange-rate changes.

Chapter 1 of this work provides an introduction to the problem of foreign-exchange risk. Chapter 2 summarizes the existing body of literature on the subject of exchange risk and direct investment. Chapter 3 is devoted to a thorough discussion of the potential impact changing exchange rates may have on the value and operations of the firm.

Although the firm can contract forward the rate of exchange, it cannot contractually fix over sufficiently long periods of time its sales levels, product prices, or the cost of inputs. The local-currency value of foreign wages and of foreign product prices are assumed to be a function of the rate of exchange. When deviations from purchasing power parity are considered, the domestic-currency value of foreign wage costs and of foreign sales revenues becomes uncertain. These values are subject to change as the exchange-rate changes, and as a result, the local-currency profit margin of the firm becomes sensitive to exchange-rate movements. This, therefore, requires the risk-sensitive firm to consider exchange risk in its investment decisions.

Several microeconomic models have been developed to simulate firm behavior under conditions of exchange risk. These models allow the firm to select the utility-maximizing levels of domestic and foreign activity. Foreign activity (the employment of foreign labor, the commitment of resources for direct investment, and the production of output) exposes the firm to exchange risks.

A series of single-period constrained and unconstrained utility-maximization models has been employed. The firm is assumed to have risk-averse preferences. This type of behavior is incorporated in the models by use of a utility function. The function is positively related to the expected value of profits and negatively related to the variance of profits.

A model is presented in chapter 4 to study the effects of exchange risk on the firm's decision to commit productive resources to the domestic and foreign markets. This model demonstrates that the firm shifts resources to the domestic or foreign market in response to increased profit incentives, and away from the foreign market as the exposure of the profit flow to exchange risk rises. Domestic capital investment is shown to be sensitive to foreign-exchange risks, benefiting when the level of risk associated with foreign direct investment rises. The total level of firm-wide capital investment and labor employment has been shown to decline as exchange risks increase.

Drawing a correspondence from the microeconomic behavior of the firm to behavior at the aggregate level, increases in exchange risk cause the equilibrium level of direct international investment to fall. This implies that domestic capital investment levels will be higher, domestic labor employment higher, and foreign labor employment lower. In the aggregate, domestic labor will benefit, foreign labor will be hurt, while foreign capital owners will benefit from the increased scarcity of locally employed capital. Domestic capital owners are disadvantaged as they accept lower returns in response to reducing exposure to the higher level of exchange risks. On a global basis, social welfare is reduced as resources are reallocated away from higher returns and toward lower but more secure returns.

Chapter 5 studies the firm's decision on the currency denomination of debt. The debt denomination decision is influenced, in part, by the risk-return profile of the firm's other assets and liabilities. Chapter 5 provides a model which allows for the simultaneous determination of the levels of domestic and foreign capital investment, domestic and foreign labor employment, and the proportion of debt to be denominated in the foreign currency.

The risks associated with the currency denomination of debt are related to other risks incurred by the firm in its foreign operations. The results of chapter 5 indicate that funds should be raised in markets where the firms' activities take place. Changes in the operating environment that cause the firm to shift activity from one market to another also cause the firm to shift the denomination of its liabilities in the same direction. The tendency to denominate debt in the currency in which productive activity takes place increases as the level of exchange risks rise.

On a macroeconomic level, the study indicates that firms will increase the proportion of total debt raised in the foreign market as exchange risks rise. Whether total credit demand increases in the foreign market is, however, uncertain since the overall level of direct investment is reduced.

In chapter 6 a model is presented which permits the flow of goods between markets. The introduction of trade allows the firm to separate its production and sales decisions. This provides the firm with greater flexibility in the optimization process. The model also permits an investigation of tariffs and the effect of exchange risk on international trade. The model produces results consistent with traditional trade theory.

The introduction of exchange-risk considerations does not affect the direction of responses to changing import tariffs. As foreign import tariffs are increased, the firm is shown to shift production to the protected foreign market, while shifting sales to the domestic market. As a result, foreign imports are shown to decrease as foreign production rises while foreign sales fall.

With trade permitted, the firm is shown to counterbalance risk and return attributes in its sales and production decisions. Factors which led the firm to reduce risks in production also result in the firm's accepting greater exposure to risk in sales, and vice-versa. Conditions which reduced expected returns in sales led the firm to increase expected returns in production, and vice versa. On a trade basis, the firm is shown to increase net exports to the market where selling conditions improve or where production conditions deteriorate.

In conclusion, the evaluation process for the firm involves three steps before decisions can be made. First, what are the firms' attitudes towards risk? What is the trade-off between exposure to risk and profitability that the firm is willing to make? Secondly, what is the potential exposure to risk from operations in foreign markets? What are the revenue risks, the operating cost risks, and the financing cost risks? Of equal importance and a major source of neglect is the question of the interrelated nature of these risks. In many instances exposure in one area may offset exposure in other areas. Along a similar line of reasoning, are there offsets between the risks associated with different foreign operations? Are the exchange risks associated with German-based operations offset to any extent by the risks incurred with French-based operations?

The last step in the evaluation process is the review of alternatives. The objective remains the same, to service a foreign market profitably, or to exploit a foreign-located cost advantage. However, there are many ways of achieving the objective, with each alternative having its associated costs, revenues and risk attributes. When this three-step evaluation process is complete, the firm is in the position to make competent direct investment decisions that reasonably incorporate exchange-risk considerations.

Appendix A

Second-Order Conditions for Utility Maximization

This appendix contains the second-order conditions for utility maximization for each of the models presented in this study.

Chapter 4: Direct Investment Model

Second-order conditions were tested by differentiating equation system 4.09 through 4.12 with respect to the endogenous variables. The following results were obtained:

$$U_{L_1 L_1} = P_1 Q_{L_1 L_1}$$

$$U_{L_1 I_1} = U_{I_1 L_1} = P_1 Q_{L_1 I_1}$$

$$U_{I_1 I_1} = P_1 Q_{I_1 I_1} - 2r'$$

$$U_{L_2 L_2} = \overline{e} P_2 Q_{L_2 L_2} - b[2 Q_2 Q_{L_2 L_2} \sigma_{ep}^2 + 2 Q_{L_2}^2 \sigma_{ep}^2$$
$$+ 2\sigma_{ew}^2 - 4 Q_{L_2} \sigma_{epew}^2 - 2 Q_{L_2 L_2} L_2 \sigma_{epew}^2]$$

$$U_{L_2 I_2} = U_{I_2 L_2} = \overline{e} P_2 Q_{L_2 I_2} - b[2 Q_{I_2} Q_{L_2} \sigma_{ep}^2$$
$$- 2 Q_{I_2} + 2 Q_2 Q_{L_2 I_2} \sigma_{ep}^2 - 2 Q_{I_2} \sigma_{epew}^2$$
$$- 2 L_2 Q_{L_2 I_2} \sigma_{epew}^2]$$

$$U_{I_2 I_2} = \overline{e} P_2 Q_{I_2 I_2} - 2r' - b[2 Q_{I_2}^2 \sigma_{ep}^2 + 2 Q_2 Q_{I_2 I_2} \sigma_{ep}^2$$
$$- 2 L_2 Q_{I_2 I_2} \sigma_{epew}^2]$$

$$U_{I_1 I_2} = U_{I_2 I_1} = -2r'$$

$$U_{L_1 L_2} = U_{L_2 L_1} = 0$$

$$U_{I_1 L_2} = U_{L_2 I_1} = 0$$

$$U_{L_1 I_2} = U_{I_2 L_1} = 0$$

After substitution, the Hessian matrix is summarized as follows:

$$|H| = \begin{vmatrix} U_{L_1L_1} & U_{L_1I_1} & 0 & 0 \\ U_{I_1L_1} & U_{I_1I_1} & 0 & U_{I_1I_2} \\ 0 & 0 & U_{L_2L_2} & U_{L_2I_2} \\ 0 & U_{I_2I_1} & U_{I_2L_2} & U_{I_2I_2} \end{vmatrix}$$

The principal minors of the Hessian matrix are as follows:

$$|H_1| = U_{L_1L_1}$$

$$|H_2| = U_{L_1L_1}U_{I_1I_1} - U_{L_1I_1}^2$$

$$|H_3| = U_{L_2L_2}|H_2|$$

$$|H_4| = |H|$$

The assumption of a strictly concave linearly homogeneous production function results in negative second-order partials, positive second-order cross-partials, and $Q_{LL}Q_{KK} > Q_{KL}^2$ for both Q_1 and Q_2. The utility function is assumed to be strictly concave in the neighborhood of a maximum resulting in determinate signs for the following principal minors:

$$|H_1| < 0$$

$$|H_2| > 0$$

$$|H_3| < 0$$

$$|H_4| = |H| > 0$$

The signs of the principal minors are then used to determine the signs of the comparative-static derivatives.

Chapter 5: Debt Denomination Model

To test the sensitivity of the equilibrium values of $I_1, I_2, L_1, L_2,$ and α to changes in the exogenous variables, Conditions 5.05 through 5.09 were differentiated totally with respect to each of the exogenous and endogenous variables. The five equations were then organized into the following equation system:

$$\left| \frac{\partial^2 U}{\partial X_i \partial X_j} \right| \left| dX_i \right| = \left| \Sigma dY_i \right|$$

where X = Endogenous variables

Y = Exogenous variables.

The matrix $\left| \partial^2 U / \partial X_i \partial X_j \right|$ is the Hessian matrix. Its elements are shown below:

$$\mathcal{L}_{L_1L_1} = P_1 Q_{L_1L_1}$$

$$\mathcal{L}_{L_1I_1} = P_1 Q_{L_1I_1}$$

$$\mathcal{L}_{L_1L_2} = \mathcal{L}_{L_1I_2} = \mathcal{L}_{L_1}\alpha = \mathcal{L}_{L_1} = 0$$

$$\mathcal{L}_{I_1I_1} = P_1 Q_{I_1I_1}$$

$$\mathcal{L}_{I_1L_2} = \mathcal{L}_{I_1I_2} = \mathcal{L}_{I_1}\alpha = 0$$

$$\mathcal{L}_{I_1}\lambda = 1$$

$$\mathcal{L}_{L_2L_2} = \overline{e}P_2 Q_{L_2L_2} - 2bQ_{L_2}Q_{L_2}\sigma_{ep}^2 - 2bQ_2 Q_{L_2L_2}\sigma_{ep}^2$$
$$\quad - 2b\sigma_{ew}^2 + 2bQ_{L_2L_2}\sigma_{epew}^2 + 2bQ_{L_2}\sigma_{epew}^2$$
$$\quad + 2bQ_{L_2}\sigma_{epew}^2 + 2bQ_{L_2L_2}r\alpha D\sigma_{epe}^2$$

$$\mathcal{L}_{L_2I_2} = \overline{e}P_2 Q_{L_2I_2} - 2bQ_{I_2}Q_{L_2}\sigma_{ep}^2 - 2bQ_2 Q_{L_2I_2}\sigma_{ep}^2$$
$$\quad + 2bQ_{L_2I_2}L_2\sigma_{epew}^2 + 2bQ_{I_2}\sigma_{epew}^2$$
$$\quad + 2bQ_{L_2I_2}r\alpha D\sigma_{epe}^2$$

$$\mathcal{L}_{L_2}\alpha = 2bQ_{L_2}rD\sigma_{epe}^2 - 2brD\sigma_{ewe}^2$$

$$\mathcal{L}_{L_2}\lambda = 0$$

$$\mathcal{L}_{I_2I_2} = \overline{e}P_2 Q_{I_2I_2} - 2bQ_{I_2}Q_{I_2}\sigma_{ep}^2 - 2bQ_2 Q_{I_2I_2}\sigma_{ep}^2$$
$$\quad + 2bQ_{I_2I_2}L_2\sigma_{epew}^2 + 2bQ_{I_2I_2}r\alpha D\sigma_{epe}^2$$

$$\mathcal{L}_{I_2}\alpha = 2bQ_{I_2}rD\sigma_{epe}^2$$

$$\mathcal{L}_{I_2}\lambda = 1$$

$$\mathcal{L}\alpha\alpha = -2br^2 D^2 \sigma_e^2$$

$$\mathcal{L}\alpha\lambda = 0$$

$$\mathcal{L}\lambda\lambda = 0$$

Cramer's Rule was used to solve for each of the comparative-static derivatives.

Chapter 6: Trade Model

Conditions 6.04 through 6.10 were differentiated totally with respect to the endogenous variables and each of the exogenous variables. The elements of the Hessian matrix are shown below:

$$\mathcal{L}_{L_1L_1} = \lambda Q_{L_1L_1}$$

$\mathcal{L}_{L_1 I_1} = \lambda Q_{L_1 I_1}$

$\mathcal{L}_{L_1} \lambda = Q_{L_1}$

$\mathcal{L}_{L_1 L_2} = \mathcal{L}_{L_1 I_2} = \mathcal{L}_{L_1 S_1} = \mathcal{L}_{L_1 S_2} = 0$

$\mathcal{L}_{I_1 I_1} = \lambda Q_{I_1 I_1} - 2r'$

$\mathcal{L}_{I_1 I_2} = -2r'$

$\mathcal{L}_{L_2 L_2} = t Q_{L_2 L_2} + \lambda Q_{L_2 L_2} - 2b\sigma_{ew}^2$

$\mathcal{L}_{L_2 I_2} = t Q_{L_2 I_2} + \lambda Q_{L_2 I_2}$

$\mathcal{L}_{L_2 S_2} = 2b\sigma_{epew}^2$

$\mathcal{L}_{L_2} \lambda = Q_{L_2}$

$\mathcal{L}_{I_1} \lambda = Q_{I_1}$

$\mathcal{L}_{L_2 S_1} = 0$

$\mathcal{L}_{I_2 I_2} = t Q_{I_2 I_2} + \lambda Q_{I_2 I_2} - 2r'$

$\mathcal{L}_{I_2} \lambda = Q_{I_2}$

$\mathcal{L}_{I_2 S_1} = \mathcal{L}_{I_2 S_2} = 0$

$\mathcal{L}_{S_1} \lambda = -1$

$\mathcal{L}_{S_1 S_1} = \mathcal{L}_{S_1 S_2} = 0$

$\mathcal{L}_{S_2 S_2} = -2b\sigma_{ep}^2$

$\mathcal{L}_{S_2} \lambda = -1$

$\mathcal{L}_{\lambda\lambda} = 0$

Appendix B

Total Derivatives

This appendix contains the total derivatives used to develop the comparative-static derivatives which are cited throughout the text of this study. To solve for any particular comparative-static derivative, divide both sides of the total derivative by the change in the particular exogenous variable, while setting all other exogenous change variables equal to zero.

The following notation has been employed in condensing the total derivatives:

Let $|H|$ = Hessian determinant

$|\bar{H}|$ = Bordered Hessian determinant

$|H_i|$ = ith principal minor subdeterminant

$|X,Y,Z|$ = A subdeterminant of the Hessian containing the X, Y, and Z endogenous variables.

Note that these symbols are redefined for each model, i.e., $|H|$ of the basic model is not equivalent to $|H|$ of the trade model.

Chapter 4

$$dL_1 = |H|^{-1}[(Q_{I_1}U_{L_1I_1}|L_2,I_2|-Q_{L_1}|I_1,L_2,I_2|)dP_1$$

$$+ |I_1,L_2,I_2|dW_1$$

$$+ (U_{L_1I_1}(U_{L_2I_2}U_{I_1I_2}-|L_2,I_2|)dr^\circ$$

$$- (U_{L_1I_1}U_{I_1I_2})\{(U_{L_2L_2}Q_{I_2}-U_{L_2I_2}Q_{L_2})d\overline{eP_2}$$

$$+ U_{L_2I_2}(d\overline{eW_2} + 4bL_2d\sigma_{ew}^2)$$

$$+ 4bQ_2(Q_{L_2}U_{L_2I_2} - Q_{I_2}U_{L_2L_2})d\sigma_{ep}^2$$

$$+ 4b(L_2U_{L_2I_2}Q_{I_2} - (Q_2+L_2Q_{L_2})U_{L_2I_2})d\sigma_{epew}^2$$

$$+ ((\partial\sigma_\pi^2/\partial L_2)U_{L_2I_2} - (\partial\sigma_\pi^2/\partial I_2)U_{L_2L_2})db\}]$$

$$dI_1 = |H|^{-1}[(|L_2,I_2|)((Q_{L_1}U_{L_1I_1} - Q_{I_1}U_{L_1L_1})dP_1$$

$$- U_{L_1I_1}dW_1)$$

$$+ (U_{L_1L_1}(|L_2,I_2| - U_{L_2L_2}U_{I_1I_2}))dr^\circ$$

$$+ (U_{L_1L_1}U_{I_1I_2})\{*\}]$$

*These terms are identical to the terms contained in { } in dL_1.

$$dL_2 = |H|^{-1}[(U_{L_2I_2}U_{I_1I_2})((Q_{L_1}U_{L_1I_1}-Q_{I_1}U_{L_1L_1})dP_1$$
$$- U_{L_1I_1}dW_1) -U_{L_2I_2} (|H_2|-U_{L_1L_1}U_{I_1I_2})dr^o$$
$$+ \{(Q_{I_2}U_{L_2I_2}|H_2|-Q_{L_2}|L_1,I_1,I_2|)(d\overline{e}\overline{P}_2-4bQ_2d\sigma_{ep}^2)$$
$$+ |L_1,I_1,I_2|(d\overline{e}\overline{W}_2+4bL_2d\sigma_{ew}^2)$$
$$+ 4b(L_2Q_{I_2}U_{L_2I_2}|H_2|-(Q_2+Q_{L_2}L_2)|L_1,I_1,I_2|)d\sigma_{epew}^2$$
$$+ ((\partial\sigma_\pi^2/\partial L_2)|L_1,I_1,I_2|-(\partial\sigma_\pi^2/\partial I_2)U_{L_2I_2}|H_2|)db\}]$$

$$dI_2 = |H|^{-1}[(U_{L_2L_2}U_{I_1I_2})((Q_{I_1}U_{L_1L_1}-Q_{L_1}U_{L_1I_1})dP_1$$
$$+ U_{L_1I_1}dW_1) +U_{L_2L_2}(|H_2|-U_{L_1L_1}U_{I_1I_2})dr^o$$
$$+ \{*\}]$$

*These terms are identical to the terms contained in { } in dL_2 when the following substitutions are made:

$$U_{L_2I_2} \ |H_2| \ \text{for} \ -|L_1,I_1,I_2|$$
$$|H_3| \ \text{for} \ -U_{L_2I_2}|H_2|$$

Chapter 5: Debt Denomination Model

The following notation has been used for this model:

$$|M_1| = \begin{vmatrix} -Q_{L_2} & \mathcal{L}_{L_2L_2} & \mathcal{L}_{L_2}\alpha \\ -Q_{I_2} & \mathcal{L}_{L_2I_2} & \mathcal{L}_{I_2}\alpha \\ 0 & \mathcal{L}_{L_2}\alpha & \mathcal{L}\alpha\alpha \end{vmatrix}$$

$$|M_2| = \begin{vmatrix} \alpha Q_{L_2} & \mathcal{L}_{L_2L_2} & \mathcal{L}_{L_2}\alpha \\ \alpha Q_{I_2} & \mathcal{L}_{L_2I_2} & \mathcal{L}_{I_2}\alpha \\ Q_2 & \mathcal{L}_{L_2}\alpha & \mathcal{L}\alpha\alpha \end{vmatrix}$$

(a) $= (\mathcal{L}_{L_2I_2}\mathcal{L}\alpha\alpha - \mathcal{L}_{I_2}\alpha\mathcal{L}_{L_2}\alpha)$

(b) $= (\mathcal{L}_{L_2L_2}\mathcal{L}_{I_2}\alpha - \mathcal{L}_{L_2I_2}\mathcal{L}_{L_2}\alpha)$

(c) $= (\mathcal{L}_{L_2I_2}\mathcal{L}_{I_2}\alpha - \mathcal{L}_{I_2I_2}\mathcal{L}_{L_2}\alpha)$

$$dL_1 = |\overline{H}|^{-1}[(Q_{L_1}|L_2,I_2,\alpha| + (Q_{L_1}\mathcal{L}_{I_1I_1} -Q_{I_1}\mathcal{L}_{L_1I_1})|L_2,\alpha|)dP_1$$
$$+ |\lambda,L_2,I_2,\alpha,I_1|dW_1$$
$$+ (\mathcal{L}_{L_1I_1}) \{ |M_1|(d\overline{e}\overline{P}_2 - 2bQ_2d\sigma_{ep}^2)$$

$$+ 2brD(|M_2|d\sigma^2_{epe} + rD(b)d\sigma^2_e)$$

$$+ (a)(d\overline{e}\overline{W}_2 + 2bL_2d\sigma^2_{ew} - 2b(L_2Q_{L_2}+Q_2)d\sigma^2_{epew}$$

$$+ 2br\alpha Dd\sigma^2_{ewe})$$

$$+ 2b|L_2,\alpha|(Q_{I_2}L_2d\sigma^2_{epew} + L_2rDd\sigma^2_{ewe})$$

$$+ |L_2,I_2,\alpha|dD\}]$$

$$dI_1 = |\overline{H}|^{-1}r_{\triangleleft}|L_2,\alpha|)((\mathcal{L}_{L_1L_1}Q_{I_1} - \mathcal{L}_{L_1I_1}Q_{L_1})dP_1$$

$$+ \mathcal{L}_{L_1I_1}dW_1)$$

$$- (\mathcal{L}_{L_1L_1})\{*\}]$$

*These terms are identical to the terms contained in { } in dL_1.

$$dL_2 = |\overline{H}|^{-1}[(a)((\mathcal{L}_{L_1L_1}Q_{I_1}-\mathcal{L}_{L_1I_1}Q_{L_1})dP_1+\mathcal{L}_{L_1I_1}dW_1)$$

$$+ (|L_1,I_1|Q_{L_2}\mathcal{L}\alpha\alpha-\mathcal{L}_{L_1L_1} (Q_{I_2}(a)-Q_{L_2}|I_2,\alpha|))(d\overline{e}\overline{P}_2$$

$$- 2bQ_2d\sigma^2_{ep}).$$

$$- (\mathcal{L}_{L_1L_1}|I_2,\alpha|+\mathcal{L}\alpha\alpha|L_1,I_1|)(d\overline{e}\overline{W}_2-2bL_2d\sigma^2_{ew})$$

$$+ (2brD)((r\alpha D) (\mathcal{L}_{L_2}\alpha|L_1,I_1|-\mathcal{L}_{L_1L_1}(c))d\sigma^2_e$$

$$+ (\mathcal{L}_{L_1L_1}|M_2|+\alpha(Q_{L_2}\mathcal{L}\alpha\alpha-Q_{I_2}\mathcal{L}_{L_2}\alpha)|L_1,I_1|)d\sigma^2_{epe}$$

$$- (\mathcal{L}_{L_1L_1}(\alpha|I_2,\alpha|+L_2(c)+|L_1,I_1|(\alpha\mathcal{L}\alpha\alpha-L_2\mathcal{L}_{L_2}\alpha))d\sigma^2_{ewe})$$

$$+ 2b(L_2Q_{L_2}+Q_2)(\mathcal{L}_{L_1L_1}|I_2,\alpha|+\mathcal{L}\alpha\alpha|L_1,I_1|$$

$$- Q_{I_2}L_2\mathcal{L}_{L_1L_1}(a)d\sigma^2_{epew}$$

$$+ |L_1I_1|(a)dD]$$

$$dI_2 = |\overline{H}|^{-1}[(|L_2,\alpha|)((\mathcal{L}_{L_1I_1}Q_{L_1}-\mathcal{L}_{L_1L_1}Q_{I_1})dP_1$$

$$- \mathcal{L}_{L_1I_1}dW_1)$$

$$+ (\mathcal{L}_{L_1L_1})(|M_1|d\overline{e}\overline{P}_2+2brD((\alpha(a)+L_2(b))d\sigma^2_{ewe}$$

$$+ rD\alpha(b)d\sigma^2_e-|M_2|d\sigma^2_{epe})$$

$$+ 2bL_2(a)d\sigma^2_{ew}$$

$$- 2b((Q_{L_2}L_2+Q_2)(a)-Q_{I_2}L_2|L_2,\alpha|)d\sigma^2_{epew}$$

$$+ (a)d\overline{e}\overline{W}_2$$

$$+ 2bQ_2(Q_{L_2}(a)-Q_{I_2}|L_2,\alpha|)d\sigma^2_{ep})$$

$$- |L_1,I_1| |L_2,\alpha|dD]$$

$$d\alpha = |\overline{H}|^{-1}[(b)(\mathcal{L}_{L_1I_1}dW_1+(\mathcal{L}_{L_1L_1}Q_{I_1}-\mathcal{L}_{L_1I_1}Q_{L_1})dP_1)$$

$$- \mathcal{L}_{L_1L_1}((Q_{I_2}(b)-Q_{L_2}(c))+Q_{L_2}\mathcal{L}_{L_2}\alpha|L_1,I_1|)(d\overline{e}\overline{P}_2$$

$$- 2bQ_2d\sigma^2_{ep})$$

$+ (\mathcal{L}_{L_2}\alpha|L_1,I_1|-\mathcal{L}_{L_1L_1}(c))(d\overline{e}\overline{W}_2+d\sigma^2_{ew})-(\alpha|r)dr^{\circ}$

$+ 2b((Q_{L_2}L_2+Q_2)(\mathcal{L}_{L_1L_1}(c)-|L_1,I_1|\mathcal{L}_{L_2}\alpha$

$- \mathcal{L}_{L_1L_1}L_2Q_{I_2}(b))d\sigma^2_{epew}$

$- 2brD((\mathcal{L}_{L_1L_1}(\alpha(c)+L_2|L_2,I_2|)-|L_1,I_1|(L_2\mathcal{L}_{L_2L_2}$

$- \alpha\mathcal{L}_{L_2}\alpha))d\sigma^2_{ewe}$

$+ r\alpha D(\mathcal{L}_{L_1L_1}|L_2,I_2|+\mathcal{L}_{L_2L_2}|L_1,I_1|)d\sigma^2_e)$

$+ 2brD\mathcal{L}_{L_1L_1}(Q_{L_2}\alpha(a-\mathcal{L}_{L_2}\alpha\mathcal{L}_{L_1L_1})-Q_{I_2}\alpha(b)$

$+ Q_2(|L_2,I_2|+\mathcal{L}_{L_1L_1}\mathcal{L}_{I_1I_1}))d\sigma^2_{epe}$

$+ (\mathcal{L}_{L_1L_1}(\alpha|D)|(L_2,I_2,\alpha|+(\alpha|D)|L_1,I_1,L_2,\alpha|$

$+ |L_1,I_1|(b))dD]$

Chapter 6

The following notation has been employed in chapter 6:

Let $\rho^2 = \sigma^4_{epew}|\sigma^2_{ep}\sigma^2_{ew}$

$$|D_1| = \begin{vmatrix} -Q_{I_1} & 0 & \mathcal{L}_{I_1I_2} & 0 \\ -Q_{L_2} & \mathcal{L}_{L_2L_2} & \mathcal{L}_{L_2I_2} & \mathcal{L}_{L_2S_2} \\ -Q_{I_2} & \mathcal{L}_{L_2I_2} & \mathcal{L}_{I_2I_2} & 0 \\ 1 & \mathcal{L}_{L_2S_2} & 0 & \mathcal{L}_{S_2S_2} \end{vmatrix}$$

$$|D_2| = \begin{vmatrix} -Q_{I_1} & \mathcal{L}_{L_1L_1} & \mathcal{L}_{L_1I_1} & 0 \\ -Q_{I_1} & \mathcal{L}_{L_1I_1} & \mathcal{L}_{I_1I_1} & \mathcal{L}_{I_1I_2} \\ -Q_{L_2} & 0 & 0 & \mathcal{L}_{L_2I_2} \\ -Q_{I_2} & 0 & \mathcal{L}_{I_1I_2} & \mathcal{L}_{I_2I_2} \end{vmatrix}$$

$$|D_3| = \begin{vmatrix} 0 & -Q_{I_1} & -Q_{L_1} & 1 \\ -Q_{L_2} & 0 & \mathcal{L}_{L_2L_2} & \mathcal{L}_{L_2S_2} \\ -Q_{I_2} & \mathcal{L}_{I_2I_2} & \mathcal{L}_{L_2I_2} & 0 \\ 1 & 0 & \mathcal{L}_{L_2S_2} & \mathcal{L}_{S_2S_2} \end{vmatrix}$$

$dL_1 = |\overline{H}|^{-1}[(Q_{L_1}|I_1,L_2,I_2,S_2|+\mathcal{L}_{L_1I_1}|D_1|)dP_1$

$+ |\lambda,I_1,L_2,I_2,S_1,S_2|dw_1$

$+ \{(\mathcal{L}_{L_1I_1}\mathcal{L}_{I_1I_2}\mathcal{L}_{L_2I_2})(\mathcal{L}_{L_2S_2}(d\overline{e}\overline{P}_2-2bS_2d\sigma^2_{ep})$

$$+ \mathcal{L}_{S_2S_2}\mathrm{de}\overline{W}_2 + 2bL_2d\sigma_{ew}^2)$$

$$+ 4bL_2(\rho^2-1)(\sigma_{ew}^2\sigma_{ep}^2)\mathrm{db}$$

$$+ 2b(L_2\mathcal{L}_{L_2S_2}-S_2\mathcal{L}_{S_2S_2})d\sigma_{epew}^2)$$

$$+ \mathcal{L}_{L_1I_1}((|L_2,I_2,S_2|-\mathcal{L}_{I_1I_2}|L_2,S_2|)\mathrm{dr}^\circ$$

$$+ \mathcal{L}_{I_1I_2}(Q_{I_2}|L_2,S_2|-\mathcal{L}_{L_2I_2}(Q_{L_2}\mathcal{L}_{S_2S_2}+\mathcal{L}_{L_2S_2}))\mathrm{dt}^\circ)\}]$$

$$\mathrm{dI}_1 = |\overline{H}|^{-1}[\mathcal{L}_{L_1I_1}|L_2,I_2,S_2|\mathrm{dW}_1-(Q_{L_1}\mathcal{L}_{L_1I_1}|L_2,I_2,S_2|$$

$$+ \mathcal{L}_{L_1L_1}|M_1|\mathrm{dP}_1$$

$$+ \{*\}]$$

*These terms are equal to the terms included in { } of dL$_1$ when $-\mathcal{L}_{L_1L_1}$ is substituted for $\mathcal{L}_{I_1I_1}$.

$$\mathrm{dL}_2 = |\overline{H}|^{-1}[(\mathcal{L}_{L_2S_2}|L_1,I_1,I_2|-\mathcal{L}_{S_2S_2}|D_2|)\mathrm{dP}_1$$

$$+ \mathcal{L}_{L_2I_1}\mathcal{L}_{I_2S_2}((|L_1,I_1|-\mathcal{L}_{L_1L_1}\mathcal{L}_{I_1I_2})\mathrm{dr}^\circ$$

$$+ \mathcal{L}_{L_1I_1}\mathcal{L}_{I_1I_2}\mathrm{dW}_1)$$

$$+ (|L_1,I_1,I_2|)(\mathcal{L}_{L_2S_2}(2bS_2d\sigma_{ep}^2-\mathcal{L}_{L_2S_2}\mathrm{de}\overline{P}_2)$$

$$+ 4bL_2(1-\rho^2)(\sigma_{ep}^2\sigma_{ew}^2)\mathrm{db}$$

$$+ 2b(S_2\mathcal{L}_{S_2S_2}-L_2\mathcal{L}_{L_2S_2})d\sigma_{epew}^2)$$

$$+ |\lambda,L_1,I_1,I_2,S_1,S_2|\mathrm{de}\overline{W}_2$$

$$- 2bL_2|L_1,I_1,I_2,S_2|d\sigma_{ew}^2$$

$$+ (Q_{L_2}|L_1,I_1,I_2,S_2|+\mathcal{L}_{L_2S_2}|L_1,I_1,I_2|$$

$$- Q_{I_2}\mathcal{L}_{L_2I_2}\mathcal{L}_{S_2S_2}|L_1,I_1|)\mathrm{dt}^\circ]$$

$$\mathrm{dI}_2 = |\overline{H}|^{-1}[((|L_1,I_1|(Q_{I_2}|L_2,S_2|-\mathcal{L}_{L_2I_2}(\mathcal{L}_{L_2S_2}+Q_{L_2}\mathcal{L}_{S_2S_2})$$

$$+ \mathcal{L}_{I_1I_2}(Q_{L_1}\mathcal{L}_{L_1I_1}-Q_{I_1}\mathcal{L}_{L_1L_1})|L_2,S_2|)\mathrm{dP}_1.$$

$$- \mathcal{L}_{L_1I_1}\mathcal{L}_{I_1I_2}|L_2,S_2|\mathrm{dW}_1$$

$$+ \mathcal{L}_{L_2I_2}|L_1,I_1|(\mathcal{L}_{L_2S_2}(\mathrm{de}\overline{P}_2-2bS_2d\sigma_{ep}^2)$$

$$+ \mathcal{L}_{S_2S_2}(\mathrm{de}\overline{W}_2+2bL_2d\sigma_{ew}^2)$$

$$+ 2b(L_2\mathcal{L}_{L_2S_2}-S_2\mathcal{L}_{S_2S_2})d\sigma_{epew}^2$$

$$- ((\partial\sigma_\pi^2/\partial L_2)\mathcal{L}_{S_2S_2}-(\partial\sigma_\pi^2/\partial S_2)\mathcal{L}_{L_2S_2})\mathrm{db})$$

$$- (Q_{I_2}|L_2,S_2|-\mathcal{L}_{L_2I_2}(Q_{L_2}\mathcal{L}_{S_2S_2}+\mathcal{L}_{L_2S_2}))|L_1,I_1|\mathrm{dt}^\circ$$

$$+ (\mathcal{L}_{L_1L_1}\mathcal{L}_{I_1I_2}|L_2,S_2|-|L_1,I_1,L_2,S_2|)\mathrm{dr}^\circ]$$

$$\mathrm{dS}_1 = |\overline{H}|^{-1}[-|\lambda,L_1,I_1,L_2,I_2,S_2|\mathrm{dP}_1$$

$$- (Q_{L_1}|I_1,L_2I_2,S_2|+\mathcal{L}_{L_1I_1}|D_2|)\mathrm{dW}_1$$

$$+ \ (|L_1,I_1,L_2,I_2|-\mathcal{L}_{L_2S_2}|D_2|)(2bS_2d\sigma_{ep}^2-d\overline{e}\overline{P}_2)$$

$$+ \ (\mathcal{L}_{S_2S_2}|D_2|-\mathcal{L}_{L_2S_2}|L_1,I_1,I_2|)(d\overline{e}\overline{W}_2+2bL_2d\sigma_{ew}^2)$$

$$- \ (|L_1,I_1||\lambda,L_2,I_2,S_2|+\mathcal{L}_{L_1L_1}\mathcal{L}_{I_1I_2}|D_3|$$

$$+ \ Q_{L_1}\mathcal{L}_{L_1I_1}\mathcal{L}_{I_1I_2}|D_4|)dt^o$$

$$+ \ ((\partial\sigma_\pi^2/\partial S_2)|L_1,I_1,L_2,I_2|-\mathcal{L}_{L_2S_2}(\partial\sigma_\pi^2/\partial L_2)|L_1,I_1,I_2|)db$$

$$+ \ ((Q_{L_1}\mathcal{L}_{L_1I_1}-Q_{I_1}\mathcal{L}_{L_1L_1})|L_2,I_2,S_2|-|L_1,I_1||D_2|)dr^o]$$

$$dS_2 \ = \ |\overline{H}|^{-1}[(\mathcal{L}_{L_2S_2}|D_2|-|L_1,I_1,L_2,I_2|)dP_1$$

$$+ \ \mathcal{L}_{L_2S_2}(\mathcal{L}_{L_2I_2}((\mathcal{L}_{I_1I_2}\mathcal{L}_{L_1L_1}-|L_1,I_1|)dr^o-\mathcal{L}_{L_1I_1}\mathcal{L}_{I_1I_2}dW_1)$$

$$+ \ |L_1,I_1,I_2|(d\overline{e}\overline{W}_2+2bL_2d\sigma_{ew}^2))$$

$$+ \ |\overline{H}_6|(2bS_2d\sigma_{ep}^2-d\overline{e}\overline{P}_2)$$

$$+ \ 2bL_2(|L_1,I_1,L_2,I_2|-\mathcal{L}_{L_2S_2}|L_1,I_1,I_2|)d\sigma_{epew}^2$$

$$+ \ (Q_{I_2}\mathcal{L}_{L_2S_2}\mathcal{L}_{L_2I_2}|L_1,I_1|-Q_{L_2}\mathcal{L}_{L_2S_2}|L_1,I_1,I_2|$$

$$- \ |L_1,I_1,L_2,I_2|)dt^o$$

$$+ \ (\mathcal{L}_{L_2S_2}(\partial\sigma_\pi^2/\partial L_2)|L_1,I_1,I_2|$$

$$- \ (\partial\sigma_\pi^2/\partial S_2)|L_1,I_1,L_2,I_2|)db]$$

Notes

Chapter 1

1. For equities, see Grauer, Litzenberger, and Stehle (1976), and Solnik (1974); for currencies, see Feldstein (1968), Leyland (1971), Folks (1973), and Eaker and Robicher (1978); and for claims, see Wihlborg (1978), Kouri (1977), and Fama and Farber (1979).

2. For trade, see Baron (1978), Hooper and Kohlhagen (1978), and Baron and Forsythe (1979); for exchange rates, see Kohlhagen (1975). Studies on corporate behavior under conditions of uncertainty are discussed further in the text.

3. See Levich and Wihlborg (1980), Soenen (1979), Jacque (1976), and Makin (1978).

4. The adoption of Financial Accounting Standards Board Statement No. 52 should alleviate much of the corporate concern over accounting exposure to exchange risk. See chapter 3 for further discussions.

5. Adler (1981) questions the conclusions drawn by Agmon and Lessard. Adler raises two issues. First, has a valid statistical test been performed such that Agmon and Lessard can conclude that stock prices reflect investors' perceptions of a diversification benefit by multinational operations? Adler argues that test procedures used by Agmon and Lessard cannot adequately test for investor recognition of corporate diversification benefits. In response, Agmon and Lessard (1981) have argued that a valid test procedure was used to offer evidence for the limited question they addressed.

    Secondly, Adler questions whether foreign direct investment by firms and portfolio investment by individuals can be considered as partial substitutes. Adler answers this question by arguing that in a perfect capital market, portfolio investment and direct investment are "apparently" perfect substitutes. Adler concludes that direct and portfolio investments are partial substitutes whenever "some market imperfection intrudes to make financial decisions relevant for value maximization."

6. The tradable goods sector includes those industries which produce for the export market and those industries which produce goods for domestic consumption that compete against imported goods.

Chapter 2

1. A preferred currency is a currency perceived to be stable or with little risk of devaluation.

2. Changes in the real or price-level adjusted exchange rate.

3. Franco Modigliani and M. H. Miller, "The Cost of Capital, Corporate Finances and the Theory of Investment," *American Economic Review* 3 (June 1958):261.

4. The shadow price is a function of the firms' discount rate, the rate of asset depreciation, and anticipated capital gains/losses on physical assets. The shadow price represents an all-inclusive marginal opportunity cost for the increased utilization of an asset.

5. The local-currency price and local-currency wage functions are mathematical relationships which describe how the local-currency price or the local-currency wage is determined. The local-currency price for example, is the dependent variable, with its value "depending" on the value of the influencing or "independent" variables. This relationship is described by the local-currency price function. When it is stated that the exchange rate is included as an argument in the local-currency product price function, it is implied that the exchange rate is an independent variable whose value, in part, determines the value of the local-currency product price.

6. These conditions require all domestic and foreign prices and costs to remain at pre-devaluation values ex post. Since prices and costs do not adjust to the exchange-rate change, there is in essence a "windfall" reduction in the cost of domestic production relative to foreign production. The domestic value of the local-currency revenue flow is unaffected by the location of production, thereby resulting in the unambiguous conclusion that the relative profitability of domestic production is enhanced by a devaluation of the domestic currency.

7. For an exposition of the Capital Asset Pricing Model, see Sharpe (1964) and Lintner (1965). For international extensions of the CAPM, see Solnik (1973, 1974), Grauer, Litzenberger, and Stehle (1976), and Fama and Farber (1979).

8. Market segmentation implies that a market for a particular commodity has been artificially separated into smaller individual markets. A fully integrated capital market is a market where the same commodity (capital) is traded in all geographic locals at the same price (the interest rate). Government restrictions, poor communications or other conditions may exist which serve to "segment" the market. When this occurs, transaction terms and prices may differ by geographic location as each of the segments of the market operate somewhat independently of each other.

9. Rates of return on foreign assets are stochastic with the specific factors affecting the distribution of returns being unspecified in the model.

Chapter 3

1. Political risks or other elements of the environment which arise when operating in different political subdivisions is a separate form of risk from that termed foreign-exchange risk.

2. Financial Accounting Standards Board, Statement of Financial Accounting Standards, No. 8 (Stamford, Connecticut: Financial Accounting Standards Board, 1975).

3. The historical exchange rate is the rate that prevailed when the original transaction took place. In the case of assets or liabilities, it is the exchange rate that prevailed when the assets or liabilities were acquired.

4. Financial Accounting Standards Board, Statement of Financial Accounting Standards, No. 52 (Stamford, Connecticut: Financial Accounting Standards Board, 1981).

5. These risks would include political risks, the threat of exchange controls, or the risk of unanticipated exchange-rate changes.

6. In the absence of risk premiums, hedging costs are limited to management costs and transaction costs.

7. This discussion is based on effects described by Dufey (1972) and Shapiro (1975).

8. The classification system used in this section is similar to that employed by Wihlborg (1978) for international financial transactions.

9. Throughout this study, the exchange rate (e) is defined as the domestic value of a unit of foreign currency. Therefore, as the exchange rate rises, the domestic currency is depreciating in value relative to the foreign currency.

10. Assuming that the wine example is typical of the price/exchange rate relationship of the goods traded between these two countries.

11. It is recognized that domestic investment is also exposed to exchange risk under the same conditions which affect investments in the foreign country. However, to clearly isolate the effects of exchange risk on the firms' decisions, domestic investment is *assumed* to be insulated from exchange risk.

Chapter 4

1. This convenient assumption eliminates any consideration of "feed-back" effects from the foreign market, such as the effect of foreign production or exchange-rate adjustments on domestic product prices.

2. A constant returns-to-scale technology is assumed for production in each market. This implies that the productivity of capital and labor remains constant when the ratio of capital to labor is held constant.

3. No explicit consideration of physical asset depreciation is made in this study.

4. A single prime (') is used to denote the first derivative of the function, and a double prime (") denotes the second derivative.

5. This assumption serves to limit the size of the firm in a perfectly competitive, constant returns-to-scale world. Without this assumption, a highly successful firm could grow infinitely large in size, within the span of a single planning period.

6. The expression $P'2(e)$ and $dP2(e)/de$ are equivalent. They are used to denote the derivative of the function $P2(e)$ with respect to changes in e. The sign of the derivative indicates the direction of change of P2 with respect to changes in e. The negative sign in this instance indicates that P2, the local-currency price, will decline when e, the exchange rate, appreciates. The derivative is also the slope of the price function, when price is plotted against the exchange rate as shown in figure 4a.

7. See Baron and Forsythe (1979) for a discussion of these arguments.

8. As Tobin (1958, pp. 75–76) demonstrated, such preferences are consistent with the maximization of the expected value of a strictly concave quadradic utility function of wealth (income or profit). This type of function has expected utility positively related to the level of expected profits and negatively related to the variance of profits. See Schoemaker (1982) for a review of expected utility models.

9. Mathematically the covariance is evaluated as follows:

$$\text{Cov}(x,y) = \sum_{i=1}^{n} \frac{(x_i - \bar{x})(y_i - \bar{y})}{n}.$$

10. The profit term for each market (π_1, π_2) actually represents cash flows from current operations, or receipts minus cash outlays. No cost is attributed to the usage of existing capital, K_1 and K_2. This is because K_1 and K_2 are assumed to be fixed and cannot be deployed in other uses. In economic terms, capital once irrevocably committed is free to the firm since its opportunity cost is zero. On an accounting and tax basis, the firm may charge earnings for the use of existing capital. The inclusion of fixed-cost terms in the profit function would not alter the conclusions of this chapter since fixed costs do not influence optimization decisions made at the margin.

11. The interest rate used in this study, r, represents the economic cost of employing a unit of new capital. In economic terms, it represents the opportunity cost of investment. In financial terms, it can be assumed that the firm rents new capital, and that the per-unit rental charge, r, covers all economic costs of utilizing a unit of capital, including physical depreciation, technological obsolescence, and the expected capital gain (loss) on the sale of the asset.

12. The parameter b (b>0) is the slope of an indifference curve in mean-variance space.

13. The first order conditions are obtained by differentiating the objective function with respect to the four endogenous arguments and setting the partial derivations equal to zero.

14. The marginal revenue product is the increment of revenue attributable to the increased use of an input (capital or labor). A condition for profit maximization is to set the level of input usage at the point where marginal revenue products are equal to marginal costs.

15. The second-order conditions for maximization are included in Appendix A for reference.

16. The first-order conditions were differentiated with respect to the endogenous variables and the exogenous variable under consideration. Cramer's rule was used to solve the comparative-static derivatives.

17. The only additional assumption needed to derive these results involves the sign of $\partial^2 U / \partial L_2 \partial I_2$. The reported results are based on an assumed positive sign for $\partial^2 U / \partial L_2 \partial I_2$, whereas a negative sign would reverse the sign or yield indeterminate results for some of the derivatives. This assumption requires foreign capital and foreign labor to be "cooperative" factors in the utility function.

18. This is demonstrated by the positive signs for:

$$\left. \frac{dL_1}{dI_1} \right|_{dr^0} \quad \text{and} \quad \left. \frac{dL_2}{dI_2} \right|_{dr^0}$$

19. As the firm attempts to conserve investment funds, it will reduce the share of the investment budget allocated to the market which, prior to the reestablishment of equilibrium, adds the least to the utility of the firm.

20. The parameter b appears in all of the comparative-static derivatives, thereby relating the magnitude of these derivatives to the relative tradeoff between risk and return.

Chapter 5

1. The terms *integrated* and *segmented* have special meanings when applied to markets. An integrated world financial market implies that all participants have equal knowledge about all aspects of the market, and all participants have equal access to the markets. For example, a French borrower is treated no differently than an American borrower in the U.S. capital market. Access is not denied nor impeded by special registration requirements, taxes, or regulations for the French borrower. When these conditions exist, the various world markets tend to combine, forming one large market. Transactions can be conducted anywhere in the market with the same results. The gold markets and the foreign exchange markets are examples of markets that are close to being fully integrated.

   When barriers exist, such as denied access, special taxes, tariffs, or other forms of controls, the markets are then considered to be segmented. Prices for similar assets may differ between markets, since transaction costs differ between markets and arbitrage is hindered. When markets are segmented, "shopping" from market to market is beneficial since prices differ between the markets, and "bargains" may be found.

2. A subsidized capital market may exist when governmental controls keep prevailing interest rates below their market-determined equilibrium levels.

3. See Stanley (1981) for a review of the literature on capital structure and the cost-of-capital for multinationals.

4. The use of a constraint condition requires the use of a Lagrangian multiplier. The problem is thereby transformed from one of unconstrained maximization to that of a constrained utility maximization problem.

5. By utilizing one choice variable to determine these two stocks, the dimensions of the model are reduced by one.

6. As discussed in the previous chapter (see note 10, chapter 4), this expression actually represents cash flow from current operations. No costs have been attributed to the use of existing capital K_1 plus K_2. The opportunity cost of using fixed capital is considered to be zero since it is presumed that the fixed capital cannot be redeployed in other uses.

   Existing debt, previously issued to finance prior capital investment, may be a concern to the firm in its present-period optimization analysis. Existing debt represents a present-period obligation which must be covered by revenues from present-period operations. The currency distribution of these obligations becomes a factor in the optimization analysis. The existence of previously issued debt will affect the equilibrium value of the endogenous variables if any of this debt is foreign-currency denominated. This will occur as the fixed level of currency obligations affects the level of risk associated with different debt denomination and foreign production level decisions.

   The existence of previously issued foreign-currency-denominated debt would not affect the comparative-static results. This occurs because previously issued debt becomes an exogenous factor in the analysis; the firm is unable to alter the level of previously issued debt. This debt is then treated as a fixed *cost* in the optimization analysis, serving only to change the *coefficients* of the risk and return variables. The existence of this debt does not introduce any new variables into the analysis.

   To verify this point, let i^o represent the interest rate at which prior debt was issued, and let F_1^o and F_2^o represent, respectively, the amount of domestic and foreign-denominated debt previously issued. The profit function (5.00) would be altered by subtracting ($i^o F_1^o$ + $\tilde{e}i^o F_2^o$). The expected-value profit function (5.01) would be altered by subtracting ($i^o F_2^o$ +

$\overline{e}i^{o}F_2^{o})$. The variance of the profit flow (5.02) would be altered by adding the following: $[(i^{o^2}F_2^{o^2} + 2\alpha rDi^{o}F_2^{o}\sigma_e^2 + 2L_2i^{o}F_2^{o}\sigma_{ewe}^2 - 2Q_2(K_2+I_2,L_2)i^{o}F_2^{o}\sigma_{epe}^2]$.

The fixed cost term $i^{o}F_1^{o}$ drops out when deriving the first-order conditions. The term $\overline{e}i^{o}F_2^{o}$ is incorporated with the other debt term, $\overline{e}\alpha rD$. The combined term $(\alpha rD + i^{o}F_2^{o})\overline{e}$ reflects a larger coefficient for $\overline{e}$. The term $(i^{o^2}F_2^{o^2} + 2\alpha rDi^{o}F_2^{o}\sigma_e^2$ is combined with the risk term for new foreign currency debt, $\alpha^2 r^2 D^2 \sigma_e^2$. The resulting term $(i^{o^2}F_2^{o^2} + 2\alpha rDi^{o}F_2^{o} + \alpha^2 r^2 D^2)\sigma_e^2$ reflects a larger coefficient for σ_e^2. In a similar fashion $2L_2i^{o}F_2^{o}\sigma_{ewe}^2$ and $2Q_2(K_2+I_2,L_2)i^{o}F_2^{o}\sigma_{epe}^2$ are combined into existing covariance terms, which are then treated as larger coefficients for σ_{epe}^2 and σ_{ewe}^2.

The larger coefficients for the risk and return terms in the objective function are reflected in the equilibrium values of the endogenous variables. They do not, however, affect the signs of the comparative-static derivatives.

7. The actual cost of financing the foreign liabilities is equal to $[e/e^{o}]\alpha rD$, where e^{o} is the beginning of period exchange rate. With no loss of generality, e^{o} is set equal to unity. Therefore, the cost of financing foreign liabilities is equal to $e\alpha rD$. It is also assumed that the price of a unit of investment is equal to unity. Otherwise, a conversion factor (price) will be necessary to convert physical units of investment into financial units of currency.

8. The firm is not required to invest all of the funds that are available. One alternative is to invest in risk-free domestic government bonds, or the firm can pay down its existing debts or reduce its borrowings. This last choice would reduce the value of D in the model.

9. As in the previous model the utility function is assumed to be concave in the neighborhood of a maximum. It is also assumed that capital and labor are cooperative in the foreign market such that $\partial^2 U/\partial L_2 \partial I_2 > 0$. Consistent with this assumption is the assumption that changes in α affect L_2 and I_2 in the same direction such that $\partial^2 U/\partial L_2 \partial \alpha$ and $\partial^2 U/\partial I_2 \partial \alpha$ are of the same sign.

10. In the previous model, a change in labor employment would produce a change in capital employment. This would alter the marginal cost of capital which would then produce a series of readjustments in the equilibrium levels of input usage.

11. A similar model was developed (not shown here) where the supply of funds to the firm was endogenously determined. The increased variability of the model led to ambiguous results unless several constraining assumptions were made. See Siegel (1981, pp. 70–86).

12. The variance and covariance terms are related to movements in the exchange rate. More directly, they are related to movements in the unit cost of foreign liabilities, er, which is influenced by movements in the exchange rate.

Chapter 6

1. The use of a constraint condition introduces a seventh endogenous variable, λ, the Lagrangian multiplier.

2. In this formulation, the tariff is treated as a specific amount applied to the physical volume of imports. When the tariff is treated as a percentage of the foreign-currency price, the domestic-currency value of the tariff becomes uncertain. This introduces an additional element of uncertainty to the analysis which produces greater ambiguity in the comparative-static results.

The formulation used in this chapter studies the effect of a non-stochastic tariff on the firm's decisions when foreign-market prices and exchange rates are uncertain.

3. Unless the firm is able to sell its excess quota allocations. In this case the quota allocations would be viewed as an asset.

4. If allocations are required for all goods, the model as presented in equations 5.01 through 5.10 can be used. If allocations are required for goods above some base level, then the tariff term

$$\{t[S_2 - Q_2(K_2+I_2,L_2)]\}$$

needs to be adjusted to reflect the exclusion of some goods from the tariff.

5. The Lagrangian is differentiated with respect to the seven endogenous variables yielding the first-order conditions listed in 6.04 through 6.10.

6. Satisfaction of the first-order conditions requires the firm to set the value of the marginal product of foreign labor equal to its marginal cost plus its marginal addition to corporate risk. Therefore, when exchange risk is a positive factor, the value of the marginal product of foreign labor exceeds its marginal cost. (See condition 6.06.)

7. Considering first-order conditions 6.08 and 6.09 simultaneously yields the following relationship:

$$P_1 = \overline{e P_2} - t - 2bS_2\sigma_{ep}^2 + 2bL_2\sigma_{epew}^2$$

Rearranging terms, we have the following:

$$2bS_2\sigma_{ep}^2 - 2bL_2\sigma_{epew}^2 = \overline{e P_2} - t - P_1$$

The left-hand term is the marginal increase in corporate risk from the additional sale of a unit of output in the foreign market. This implies that $\overline{e P_2} - t - P_1 > 0$ or that $\overline{e P_2} - t > P_1$. Therefore, marginal revenue net of tariffs is higher in the foreign market.

8. In equilibrium, foreign production is more profitable than domestic production on an expected value basis. (See footnote 6.) Therefore, shifting production to the foreign market increases expected profits (and exposure to risk).

9. The direction of change in total sales levels was developed by combining the derivatives of S_1 and of S_2, taken with respect to each of the exogenous variables under consideration. The direction of change in the level of net exports was developed by comparing the direction of change in foreign sales levels to the direction of change in foreign input usage for each of these variables.

10. These conditions are defined by a negative covariance between σ_{ep}^2 and σ_{ew}^2 and large values of σ_{ep}^2 and σ_{ew}^2.

Bibliography

Adler, Michael. "Investor Recognition of Corporation International Diversification: Comment." *Journal of Finance* (March 1981).

Aggarwal, Raj. "FASB No. 8 and Reported Results of Multinational Operations: Hazard for Managers and Investors." *Journal of Accounting, Auditing, and Finance* (Spring 1978).

_____. *International Business Finance. A Selected Bibliography*. Business Research Center, University of Toledo, 1977.

Agmon, Tamir, and Lessard, Donald. "Investor Recognition of Corporate International Diversification: Reply [to Adler]." *Journal of Finance* (March 1981).

Aliber, Robert Z. "A Theory of Direct Foreign Investment." In *International Corporation: A Symposium*, pp. 17-34. Edited by Charles D. Kindleberger. Cambridge: M.I.T. Press, 1970.

_____. "Exchange Risk, Yield Curves, and the Pattern of Capital Flows." *The Journal of Finance* (1970).

_____. "The Multinational Enterprise in a Multiple Currency World." In *The Multinational Enterprise*, pp. 49-60. Edited by John M. Dunning. New York: Praeger Publishers, 1971.

_____. *Exchange Risk and Corporate International Finance*. New York: Halsted Press, 1978.

Baron, David P. "Flexible Exchange Rates, Forward Markets, and the Level of Trade." *American Economic Review* 66 (June 1978):253-66.

_____ and Forsythe, R. "Model of the Firm and International Trade under Uncertainty." *American Economic Review* (September 1979).

Batra, R. N., and Ramachandran, R. "Multinational Firms and the Theory of International Trade and Investment." *The American Economic Review* 70 (June 1980):278-90.

Calderon-Rossel, Jorge Rafael. "A Multinational Firm Sourcing Model." Ph.D. dissertation, University of Michigan, 1978.

Cohn, Richard A., and Pringle, John J. "Imperfections in International Financial Markets: Implications for Risk Premia and the Cost of Capital to Firms." *Journal of Finance* (March 1973).

Dornbusch, Rudiger. "PPP Exchange-Rate Rules and Macroeconomic Stability." *Journal of Political Economy* (January 1982).

Dufey, Gunter. "Corporate Finance and Exchange Rate Variations." *Financial Management* (Summer 1972).

_____, and Giddy, Ian. *The International Money Market*. Englewood Cliffs, N.J.: Prentice-Hall, 1978.

_____, and Giddy, Ian. "Innovation in the International Financial Markets." *Journal of International Business Studies* (Fall 1981):33–51.

Eaker, Mark R., and Robicher, Alexander A. "Foreign Exchange Hedging and the Capital Asset Pricing Model." *Journal of Finance* 33 (June 1978):1011-18.

Errunza, Vihang. "Gains from Portfolio Diversification into Less Developed Countries' Securities." *Journal of International Business Studies* (Winter 1977).

Fama, E. F., and Farber, A. "Money, Bonds, and Foreign Exchange." *The American Economic Review* 69 (September 1979):639-49.

Feldstein, Martin S. "Uncertainty and Forward Exchange Speculation." *The Review of Economics and Statistics* 50 (May 1968):182-92.

Financial Accounting Standards Board. *Statement of Financial Accounting Standards No. 8: Accounting for the Translation of Foreign Currency Transactions and Foreign Currency Financial Statements.* Stamford: FASB, 1975.

————. *Statement of Financial Accounting Standards No. 52: Foreign Currency Translations.* Stamford: FASB, 1981.

Folks, William R., Jr. "The Optimal Level of Forward Exchange Transactions." *Journal of Financial and Quantitative Analysis* 8 (January 1973):105-10.

Friedman, Milton, and Savage, L. J. "The Utility Analysis of Choices Involving Risk." *Journal of Political Economy* (August 1948).

Giddy, Ian. "Exchange Risk: Whose View?" *Financial Management* (Summer 1977).

Goehle, Donna G. *Decision Making in Multinational Corporations.* Ann Arbor: UMI Research Press, 1980.

Grauer, F. L. A., Litzenberger, R. H., and Stehle, R. E. "Sharing Rules and Equilibrium in an International Capital Market under Uncertainty." *Journal of Financial Economics* 3 (1976):233-56.

Grubel, Herbert. *Forward Exchange Speculation and the International Flow of Capital.* Stanford: Stanford University Press, 1966.

————. "Internationally Diversified Portfolios: Welfare Gains and Capital Flows." *American Economic Review* (December 1968).

Hartman, David G. "Foreign Investment and Finance with Risk." *Quarterly Journal of Economics* (May 1979):213-32

Heckerman, Donald. "The Exchange Risks of Foreign Operations." *Journal of Business* (January 1972):42-48.

Hooper, Peter, and Kohlhagen, Steven. "The Effects of Exchange Rate Uncertainty on the Prices and Value of International Trade." *Journal of International Economics* (1978):483-511.

Hughes, John S., Logue, Dennis E., and Sweeney, Richard J. "Corporate International Diversification and Market Assigned Measures of Risk and Diversification." *Journal of Financial and Quantitative Analysis* (November 1975).

Itagaki, Takao. "Systems of Taxation of Multinational Firms under Exchange Risk."

Jacque, Laurent. *Management of Foreign Exchange Risk.* Lexington, Mass : Lexington Books, 1978.

————. "Management of Foreign Exchange Risk: A Review Article." *Journal of International Business Studies* (Spring/Summer 1981).

Jacquillat, B., and Solnik, B. H. "Multinationals are Poor Tools for Diversification." *Journal of Portfolio Management* (Winter 1978).

Jean, William. *The Analytical Theory of Finance.* New York: Holt, Rinehart & Winston, 1970.

Jilling, Michael. *Foreign Exchange Risk Management in U.S. Multinationals.* Ann Arbor: UMI Research Press, 1978.

Jucker, James V., and de Faro, Clovis. "The Selection of International Borrowing Sources." *Journal of Financial and Quantitative Analysis* (September 1975).

Khandker, A. Wahhab. "Multinational Firms and the Theory of International Trade and Investment: A Correction and a Stronger Conclusion." *American Economic Review* (June 1981).

Kohlhagen, Steven, W. "The Performance of the Foreign Exchange Markets: 1971-1974." *Journal of International Business Studies* (Fall 1975).

_____. "The Effects of Exchange Rate Adjustment on International Investment—Comment." In *The Effects of Exchange Rate Adjustments*. Washington, D.C.: U.S. Printing Office, 1977a.

_____. "Exchange Rate Changes, Profitability, and Direct Foreign Investment." *Southern Economic Journal* (1981):43-52.

Kouri, Pentti J. K. "International Investment and Interest Rate Exchanges under Flexible Exchange Rates." In *The Political Economy of Monetary Reform*, pp. 74-96. Edited by Robert Z. Aliber. Montclair, N.J.: Allanheld, Osmun and Co., 1977.

Lessard, Donald. "World, National, and Industry Factors in Equity Returns." *Journal of Finance* (May 1974).

Levich, Richard M., and Wihlborg, Clas G. *Exchange Risk and Exposure*. Lexington, Mass.: Lexington Books, 1980.

Levy, H., and Markowitz, H. M. "Approximating Expected Utility by a Function of Mean and Variance." *The American Economic Review* 69 (June 1979):308-17.

_____, and Sarnat, M. "International Diversification of Investment Portfolios." *American Economic Review* (September 1970).

Lietaer, Bernard. "Managing Risks in Foreign Exchange." *Harvard Business Review* (March-April 1970):127-38.

_____. *Financial Management of Foreign Exchange*. Cambridge: M.I.T. Press, 1971.

Logue, Dennis E., and Oldfield, George S. "Managing Foreign Assets When Foreign Exchange Markets are Efficient." *Financial Management* (Summer 1977):16-22.

_____, and Willett, Thomas D. "The Effects of Exchange Rate Adjustment on International Investment." In *The Effects of Exchange Rate Adjustment*. Edited by Peter B. Clark, Dennis Logue, and Richard Sweeney. Washington, D.C.: U.S. Printing Office, 1977.

Makin, John. "Portfolio Theory and the Problem of Foreign Exchange Risk." *Journal of Finance* 33 (May 1978):517-34.

Markowitz, H. "Portfolio Selection." *Journal of Finance* (March 1952).

_____. *Portfolio Selections: Efficient Diversification of Investments*. New York: John Wiley & Sons, 1959.

Mehra, Rajnish. "On the Financing and Investment Decisions of Multinational Firms in the Presence of Exchange Risk." *Journal of Financial and Quantitative Analysis* (June 1978):227-44.

Officer, Lawrence H. "The Purchasing-Power-Parity Theory of Exchange Rates: A Review Article." *International Monetary Fund Staff Papers* 23 (March 1976):1-60.

Prindl, Andreas R. *Foreign Exchange Risk*. New York: John Wiley & Sons, 1976.

Ragazzi, Giorgio. "Theories of the Determinants of Direct Foreign Investment." *International Monetary Fund Staff Papers*.

Rodriguez, Rita. "Management of Foreign Exchange Risk in the U.S. Multi-nationals." *Journal of Financial and Quantitative Analysis* (1974).

Rugman, Alan M. *International Diversification and the Multinational Enterprise*. Lexington, Mass.: Lexington Books, 1980.

Schoemaker, Paul J. H. "The Expected Utility Model: Its Variants, Purposes, Evidence and Limitations." *Journal of Economic Literature* (June 1982).

Shapiro, Alan. "Defining Exchange Risk." *Journal of Business* (January 1977).

_____. "Capital Budgeting for the Multi-national Corporation." *Financial Management* (Spring 1978).

_____. *Foreign Exchange Risk Management*. American Management Association, 1978.

_____. "Exchange Rate Changes, Inflation, and the Value of the Multinational Corporation." *Journal of Finance* 30 (May 1975):485-502.

_____. "Capital Asset Prices: A Theory of Market Equilibrium under Conditions of Risk."

Journal of Finance (September 1964).

——, and Rubetberg, David P. "Managing Exchange Risks in a Floating World." *Financial Management* (Summer 1976):48-57.

Siegel, Michael Howard. Foreign Exchange Risk and Direct International Investment. Unpublished doctoral dissertation, University of Michigan, Ann Arbor, Michigan, 1981.

Soenen, Luc A. *Foreign Exchange Exposure Management: A Portfolio Approach.* The Netherlands: Sijthoff and Noordhoff, 1979.

Solnik, Bruno H. "Why Not Diversify Internationally Rather Than Domestically?" *Financial Analysts Journal* (July-August 1974).

——. *European Capital Markets: Towards a General Theory of International Investment.* Lexington, Mass.: Lexington Books, 1973.

——. "An Equilibrium Model of the International Capital Market." *Journal of Economic Theory* (August 1974):500-24.

Stanley, Marjorie Thines. "Capital Structure and Cost-of-Capital for the Multinational Firm." *Journal of International Business Studies* (Spring/Summer 1981).

Stevens, Guy V. G. "The Effects of Exchange Rate Adjustment on International Investment—Comment." In *The Effects of Exchange Rate Adjustments*, pp. 183-89. Edited by Peter B. Clark, Dennis Logue, and Richard Sweeney. Washington, D.C.: U.S. Printing Office, 1977.

——. "Capital Mobility and the International Firm." In *International Mobility and the Movement of Capital*, pp. 323-66. Edited by F. Machlup, W. S. Salant, and L. Tarshis. New York: National Bureau of Economic Research, 1972.

Tobin, J. E. "Liquidity Preference as Behavior Towards Risk." *Review of Economic Studies* (February 1958).

——. "The Theory of Portfolio Selection." In *The Theory of Interest Rates*. Edited by F. Hahn and F. P. R. Brechling. New York: Macmillan, 1965.

Tran, Vinh Quang. *Foreign Exchange Management in Multinational Firms.* Ann Arbor: UMI Research Press, 1978.

Wihlborg, Clas. "Currency Risks in International Financial Markets." *Princeton Studies in International Finance* 44 (1978).

Williamson, Oliver E. "The Modern Corporation: Origins, Evolution, Attributes." *Journal of Economic Literature* (December 1981).

Index

Accounting
  risk, 3, 5, 12, 15-17
Aggarwal, Raj, 16
Agmon, Tamir, 4
Aliber, Robert Z., 7, 8
Arbitrage, 42
Asset, 16, 17, 69
  existing, 44
  expected return on, 42
  financial, 12, 42
  fixed, 17, 44, 45
  foreign, 25, 30
  foreign-currency denominated, 16, 67
  functional currency, 17
  location of, 50
  long-term, 19
  real, 12, 28, 30, 39, 42-43, 51
Autarky, 53, 60

Balance of payments, 1, 2, 6, 67
Borrowing, 13, 42, 45
Bretten Woods Agreement, 1, 2
Business cycle, 2, 5

Calderon-Rossel, Jorge Rafael, 12-13
Canada, 1
Capital
  cost of, 7, 8, 29, 32-34, 36-37, 42, 45, 49, 51, 54,
    64
  existing, 28
  financial, 43-44, 49, 51
  investment, 27, 34, 35, 37, 41, 43-45, 49, 50,
    53, 57, 64, 68, 69
  marginal cost of, 57
  marginal product of, 57
  marginal revenue product of, 34, 35, 48, 49
  per-unit cost of (r), 28, 44
  physical (K), 27, 57
  proportion to be raised in the foreign market
    (α), 43, 48, 49, 50
Capital Asset Pricing Model (CAPM), 3, 11, 12,
  39, 42

Capital gains and losses, 8
Capital-labor ratio, 29
Capital-market theory, 4
Capital supply function, 35-38, 44, 60, 64
Cash flow, 39, 44, 67
Comparative static
  analysis, 35-38
  derivatives, 35, 38, 51
  endogenous variables, 35, 36, 49, 58
  exogenous variables, 35, 49
  results, 49-51, 58-66
Competition, 8, 9, 22, 23, 58, 59, 61
  international, 2, 67
  import, 9, 21
Constraint condition, 44, 47, 49, 55
Costs, 30, 34, 54
  domestic wage, 36
  financing, 45, 46, 50, 51, 52
  fixed, 51
  local-currency, 8, 9, 42, 43
  marginal, 34, 35, 57
  wage, 46, 51
Cross-hauling, 7
Currency
  adjustment, 10, 24
  appreciating, 5, 11, 12, 60
  controls, 55, 64
  convertability, 7
  denomination, 3, 15, 18, 41, 44, 51, 69
  depreciating, 5, 21, 22, 24
  devaluation, 8, 10, 20, 42
  domestic, 15, 18, 21, 22, 23, 27, 29, 30, 33, 42,
    46, 50, 58, 68
  exchange value, 2
  foreign, 10, 13, 15-18, 21-24, 29, 31, 32, 43, 45,
    46, 47, 50, 55, 60, 68
  foreign return, 12
  functional, 17
  holdings, 2, 3
  movements, 13
  of consumption, 11
  preferred, 7

price, 21
purchasing power, 20
realignment, 9
value, 21

Debt
currency denomination of, 41-52, 69
denomination decision, 3, 69
foreign, 17, 52
foreign-currency-denominated, 13, 19, 27, 46
long-term, 17
value of, 2
Decision model, 33
Direct investment, 3, 4, 6, 7, 8, 10, 25, 27, 38, 39,
43, 53, 57, 64, 68, 69
decisions, 13, 27-39, 70
location of, 10
Dividends, 44
Dufey, Gunter, 8-9

Economic
exposure, 4, 5, 16, 19, 46, 67
risk, 15, 19, 20, 25
Equities, 3
Errunza, Vihang, 4
Exchange rate, 2, 5, 9, 12, 13, 16, 18, 22, 23, 25,
33, 35, 38, 39, 42, 43, 68
in the model (e), 29
changes in, 3, 5, 7, 9, 12, 13, 14, 15, 16, 17, 19-
20, 21, 24, 25, 27, 33, 38, 39, 42, 45, 46,
50, 52, 58, 67, 68
current, 17
end-of-period, 12, 13, 14
fixed, 3, 41
floating, 2
import, 55
level of, 10
official, 55
real, 5, 6, 25
stability, 7
uncertainty, 12
volitility, 2
Exchange risk, 2-4, 6, 7, 10, 11, 13, 15-25, 27, 34,
37-39, 50-51, 54, 57, 58, 60, 65, 67, 68-69, 70
and the investment decision, 27-39
and international trade, 53-66
classification, 15
economic, 25, 46
exposure, 3, 5-6, 14, 18, 19, 50, 55, 60, 62, 66,
67
nutralized, 13
premium, 12
real, 12
Exchange risk and direct investment, model of,
7-14
Export, 5, 64, 66
net, 60, 63, 65, 66, 70
of production, 3, 10

Factor employment, 21, 36, 38
foreign, 36
total, 37, 38
de Faro, Clovis, 42
Financial Accounting Standards Board
(FASB)
Statement no. 8, 16, 17
Statement no. 52, 17, 18
Fisher effect, 45
Funds, cost and supply of, 49
Future spot rate, 18

Germany, 1
Giddy, Ian, 17
Gold, 1
Goods, 55
cost of capital, 37
non-tradable, 24
value of, 2
weighted basket of, 24
Government
constraints, 4
obligations, 3
Grubel, Herbert, 4

Hartman, David G., 13, 50
Heckerman, Donald, 8
Host-country, 27
firm, 7-8
Hughes, John S., 4

Import, 5, 55, 57, 64, 65, 66, 69
competition, 9, 19, 68
gap, 64
quota, 55
Income
effects, 30, 68
foreign-currency-denominated, 8
gross, 20
real, 5, 8, 67
sensitivity, 25
Inflation, 2, 9, 24
Input, 21, 58-61, 64, 68
level of, 28-36, 49, 53
level of labor (L_2), 33
local currency price of labor (W_2), 29
locally sourced, 58
non-capital, 28
stocks, 34
Interest rates, 2, 35, 37, 45
International Monetary Fund (IMF), 1
Inventory, 2, 17, 41, 54
Investment, 28, 31, 49, 68, 69
cost of in the second market (rI_2), 33
direct foreign, 13, 25, 38-39, 43, 48, 50, 51
diversification of, 25
domestic, 5, 13, 36, 37, 38, 39, 57
financing of, 43

foreign, 5, 7, 9, 13, 35, 37, 39, 50, 57
   level of, 37, 38, 43, 47
   level of capital (K), 28
   level of new (I), 28, 37
   marginal product of foreign, 57
   model, 35, 36
   physical, 41, 44
   real capital, 42
   return on, 3, 11, 12, 65
Investor, 4, 8, 11, 13, 28, 31, 44

Japan, 1
Jucker, James V., 42

Kohlhagen, Steven W., 10

Labor, 21, 27, 28, 37, 38, 58
   costs, 37, 45, 65
   domestic (L_1), 34, 43, 48, 57
   employment, 49, 50, 51, 53, 57, 63, 64, 68, 69
   foreign, 35, 43, 48, 51, 52, 57, 63, 64, 68, 69
   level of usage, 33, 35, 37, 38, 43
   marginal costs of (W_1), 34, 35, 48, 57
   marginal product of, 57
   marginal revenue product of ($P_1Q_{L_1}$), 34, 48
   untrained, 29
Lessard, Donald, 4
Level of available funds (D), 44, 47
Levy, H., 4
Liabilities, 16, 17, 41, 43, 45, 50, 51, 69
   currency denomination of, 51, 69
   foreign, 25, 47, 50, 52
   foreign-currency denominated, 16, 19, 43, 46, 48, 50, 51, 67
   functional currency, 17
   location of, 50
   structure of, 44
   tariff, 57
Logue, Dennis E., 4, 9-10

Marginal revenue, 56
   product, 9
Market, 3, 5, 36, 37, 42, 44, 54, 58, 64, 65, 66, 67, 69
   capital, 8, 21, 30, 42
   domestic, 5, 9, 11, 24, 27, 30, 37-38, 45, 48, 49, 50, 51, 53, 54, 58, 60-63, 64-65, 68, 69
   export, 5, 7, 9, 19, 21, 67
   financial, 1, 42, 67
   foreign, 4, 7, 8, 19, 25, 27, 32, 33, 37, 38, 45, 48, 49, 50, 51, 53, 54, 56-66, 68, 69-70
   foreign exchange, 2, 3, 18
   forward, 13
   futures, 13
   input, 15, 24, 39, 58
   output, 15, 24, 39
   world, 5, 19, 21, 24, 68
Markowitz, H., 4, 30

Mehra, Rajnish, 12, 42
Model, 6, 10, 13, 27-39, 64, 66
   activity and sales variables, 64
   decision, 33
   decision variables, 43, 48, 64
   entrepreneurial, 30
   first-order conditions, 34-35, 48-49, 51, 56-58
   foreign debt, 52
   microeconomic, 68
   risk term in, 55
   single-period, 54, 68
   symbol key, 32
   two-country, 37
   uncertainty, 38
Modigliani-Miller theorem, 8, 9, 42
Multinational firm, 3, 4, 8, 16, 37, 42, 53, 67, 68
   accounting procedures, 16
   balance sheet, 5, 15, 16, 17
   capital budget, 28, 47
   cash flow, 15, 30, 67
   competitive position, 2
   consolidated quarterly financial statement, 17
   contracts, 5
   contractual flow, 15
   cost flow, 5, 44
   debt denomination decision, 3, 41, 69
   decision process, 12
   direct investment decision, 13, 70
   earnings, 8
   export decision, 14
   financial aspects, 3, 13
   financial decision, 6, 8, 9, 12, 14, 41-42, 43
   financial structure, 15
   investment analysis, 25
   investment decision, 3, 4, 6, 7, 8, 11-12, 16, 19, 22, 25, 30, 33, 38, 39, 42, 43, 49, 53, 54, 68
   local currency cost, 9
   local currency profit margin, 19, 20, 25
   location of, 50
   market, 5, 6, 21
   model of, 38
   net income, 16
   operational decision, 7, 19
   operations, 2-3, 4, 5, 6, 8, 9, 14, 15, 17, 58, 68
   physical capacity, 29
   production decision, 53, 54, 58, 62, 66, 69, 70
   production/export decision, 3, 6
   profitability, 3, 10, 13, 31, 36, 54, 58, 60, 63, 64
   quarterly income, 18
   rate of expansion, 28, 29
   real assets, 9
   revenue and cost structure, 19, 67
   revenue flow, 5, 44
   revenue function, 9
   sales decision, 53, 54, 57, 58, 63, 66, 69
   shareholders, 4

sourcing and sales decision, 12
trade decision, 6
value of, 2, 3, 4, 6, 8, 9, 14, 15, 67, 68

Nixon, Richard M., 1
Non-tradable goods sector, 5, 21

Objective function, 47
Output, 27, 68
domestic (Q_1), 36
domestic price of (P_1), 36, 60
expected price of, 36
foreign, 57-58, 64
level of, 28
local currency price of (P_2), 29, 30
total, 53, 57
unit of, 22

Parametric solutions, 35
Payables, 16
Portfolio, 5, 9, 13, 30
diversified, 4
financial, 9
foreign assets in, 4, 30
optimal, 35
real asset, 9, 34
rebalancing, 9
return on market, 11
risk-return characteristics, 5, 9, 13, 43
selection of, 4, 43
theory, 4
world market, 12
Portfolio model, 12, 35, 38, 43
two-country, two-asset, 3
Portfolio selection model, 42
Price, 13, 29, 30, 36, 39, 46, 49, 56, 60, 62, 65, 68
domestic selling (P_1), 35, 36
elasticity of substitution, 25
foreign, 20, 21, 32, 35, 37-38, 58, 60, 64, 65
foreign output, 23
foreign selling, 65
level, 19, 20, 24
local-currency, 15, 22, 32, 33, 38, 43
local-currency product, 9, 14, 21
market, 11, 42, 55
relative, 5, 13, 24, 25, 30
of substitutes, 25
transaction, 15
translated, 20, 33, 39
Pricing relationship, 11
Prindl, Andreas R., 16
Production, 21, 28, 36, 37, 38, 42, 47, 53, 54, 60, 63, 64, 65, 66
domestic, 10, 54
export, 3
firm-wide, 54, 55

foreign, 3, 10, 19, 36, 54, 55, 57-58, 60, 62, 64, 65, 67, 69
level, 20, 27, 33, 34, 36, 51, 55, 65
surplus, 54
technology, 2
Production function, 28, 35
level of capital investment (K), 28
level of inputs, 28
level of labor employment (L), 28
level of new investment (I), 28
level of output (Q), 28
Profit, 3, 20, 30, 31, 45, 51, 54, 60, 65, 68
in the second market, 33
corporate, 46, 54
equation, 32
expected utility of, 35
local currency, 21
margin, 22, 24, 25
net, 12
translated value, 20, 21
variance of, 12, 32, 33, 34, 35, 68
Profit flow, 33, 55, 68
expected value of, 32, 45
local-currency, 42
variance of, 46
Profit function, 38, 54
for the domestic market, 32
total revenue, 32
wage bill, 32, 33
Purchasing power parity (PPP), 30, 43, 54, 67
deviations from, 20-24, 67, 68

Raw materials, 21, 28
Real income effect, 25
Receivables, 16
Resource, 2, 7, 50, 68, 73
Revenue conditions, 60
Revenue function, 10
Risk, 3, 65
accounting, 3, 15, 16
business, 27
corporate, 48, 49, 50, 52, 57, 63
corporate exposure to, 46
economic, 15
expression, 47
financial, 42
foreign-exchange, 5
from foreign-currency denominated
financial liabilities, 46
from foreign revenues, 46
from foreign wage liabilities, 46
internal price of, 19
market price of, 11, 19
operating, 24
overall, 51
political, 5

premiums, 18
production, 66
term, 55, 57
transaction, 16, 18-19
translation, 16-17
Risk-averse
behavior, 30, 43, 65
firm, 37, 62, 68
investor, 3, 13
measure of (b), 33, 38, 64
Risk-free, 3
rate of return, 11
Risk preference parameter (b), 64
Risk-premium, 35
Rugman, Alan M., 4

Sales, 54, 59, 60, 61, 62, 63, 64, 65
domestic value of foreign, 54
end-of-period rate, 14
foreign, 54, 55, 56-57, 64, 65, 66, 68
level, 19, 27, 55, 56, 63, 64, 65, 68
real, 13
revenue, 17
total, 55, 57, 60, 64-65
unit, 20
Sarnat, M., 4
Segmentation
capital market, 11
world, 41
Shadow price, 9
Shapiro, Alan, 9
Shareholder's equity, 18
Social welfare, 73
Solnik, Bruno H.,
Source-country, 27
firm, 7, 8
Stevens, Guy V., 8, 9, 10, 42
Stock, 43, 45, 53, 63
input, 34
prices, 17
value of, 15

Subsidiary, 20, 21, 25
domestic, 10
foreign, 10, 21
Substitution effects, 25
Supply of funds function, 44
Sweeny, Richard J., 4

Tariff, 54, 55, 56, 57, 65, 66, 69
policy, 53, 64
rates, 64, 66
term (t), 54
Tax, 8, 9, 54, 64
depreciation schedules, 24
income, 13
Technology, 37
Tradable goods sector, 5, 21, 25
Trade, 3, 53, 62, 64, 65-66, 69
model, 53-56, 58, 60, 62
risk, 54
theory, 64, 66, 69
Transaction risk, 18-19
Translation, 16-17
foreign-currency income, 46
gains and losses, 17
risk, 20

United States, 1, 10
dollar, 1, 10, 12, 20
Utility function, 30, 33-34, 38, 56, 68

Variance term, 33, 37, 55

Wage, 13, 39, 46, 49, 63
bargaining power, 25
bill, 32, 33, 54, 55, 58
costs, 35, 36, 37, 46, 51
foreign, 23, 32, 35, 37-38, 46, 58, 63, 65, 68
local-currency, 9, 38
local rate (W_2), 33
translated, 33, 39
Willett, Thomas D., 9, 10
Wuster, 11, 12, 42